THE DA  K

WILLIAM DOUGLAS HOME

SAMUEL FRENCH

LONDON
NEW YORK TORONTO SYDNEY HOLLYWOOD

ISBN 978-0-573-11093-1

www.samuelfrench.co.uk
www.samuelfrench.com

I read the Dame of Sark's autobiography some years ago and made a mental note that I would like to write a play about the wartime occupation of her island by the Germans. This spring I wrote asking for her blessing and enquiring whether she would let me use her name or if she would prefer that I should fictionalise the story. She replied that she would like to read the play before deciding. I sent it to her during the first week in June. On 11th June she wrote back: "Dear Mr Douglas Home, I do not see anything that would be disagreeable to me in letting my name be used in your play." She went on, "Would you care to come and spend a couple of days with me?" Alas, the sad news of her death came ten days before my wife and I, our two young children and Celia Johnson were due to call on her. Charles Hickman, however, who had been over earlier to photograph the room in which the play is set, had a long and fruitful conversation with her. He also met Cecile, now in her late seventies. I made one promise to the Dame, which was that I would put a note in the programme to the effect that although Major Lanz and Dr Braun were indeed the first two German officers to land on Sark, they did not in fact remain there throughout the war (as they do in the play for dramatic convenience) but were replaced by other officers of similar character and rank. "I like your idea of a note in the programme," she wrote. "It will spare me masses of letters pointing out that they had gone by Christmas 1940." The period of Colonel von Schmettau's sojourn in the Channel Islands was exactly as depicted in the play.

William Douglas Home

BBC News Broadcast

At the beginning of each scene (except Scene 6) there is a short radio announcement. These announcements should be heard on the front-of-house speakers with the footlights lighting the Curtain.

Enquiries regarding recordings of the speeches should be made to Samuel French Ltd.

THE DAME OF SARK

An Oxford Theatre Festival Production, first presented at Wyndham's Theatre, London, by Ray Cooney on the 17th October 1974, with the following cast of characters:

Bob Hathaway	Alan Gifford
Sibyl Hathaway	Celia Johnson
Cecile	Jill Raymond
Major Lanz	John Pennington
Dr Braun	Nicholas Loukes
Colonel von Schmettau	Tony Britton
Wilhelm Muller	Peter Settelen
Colonel Graham	Nicholas Courtney
Jim Robinson	Hugh Wooldridge
Mr Bishop	Martin Carroll
Mrs Bishop	Brenda Duncan
The Cowman	Scott Taylor

The play directed by Charles Hickman
Setting by Anthony Holland

The action takes place in the drawing-room of the Seigneurie on Sark

SCENE 1	1940	Summer
SCENE 2	1941	Spring
SCENE 3	1942	Autumn
SCENE 4	1943	Winter
SCENE 5	1944	Summer
SCENE 6	1945	Summer

Period—the Second World War

PRELUDE TO SCENE 1

This is the BBC Home Service. Here is the first news for today, Monday the first of July nineteen forty, and this is Alvar Lidell reading it.

Early this morning two enemy aircraft were shot down over this country, and an enemy seaplane was brought down over the North-East coast. Our bombers have continued their raids on Germany and our fighters have had successes over France. There have also been successful air operations in Africa. The Russian occupation of Rumanian territory continues.

The following statement has just come in from the Ministry of Information:

The Channel Islands have been demilitarised. It is learned that enemy landings have been made in Jersey and Guernsey. Telegraphic and telephonic communications have been cut, and no further information is at present available.

In a communiqué which reached us half an hour ago, the RAF...

SCENE 1

The drawing-room of the Seigneurie on Sark. Summer, 1940

There are doors leading to the hall and the rest of the house, and to the study; french windows to the garden, from which there is a view of the drive; a fireplace with firestool. (See plan on page 55)

When the CURTAIN rises, a charming man is discovered sitting, smoking his pipe, playing patience. He is in his fifties. The door opens and his wife comes in. She is about the same age—firm, good-looking and determined, with no fuss about her

Sibyl They'll be here in ten minutes.

Bob Good for them. Maybe I'll have got this out by then.

Sibyl Do you realize this is the first time an enemy has set foot on British soil since William the Conqueror?

Bob And he came from round here, the bastard, didn't he?

Sibyl How can you be so calm?

Bob Could be because I'm neutral.

Sibyl You'll never get away with that!

Bob No? You just watch me, honey! After all, why shouldn't I? I'm an American as plain as plain. And they're not to know that I was naturalized in nineteen-nineteen. They've a lot on their hands just at present.

Sibyl They'll find out in the end.

Bob I daresay. But until they do, it'll maybe help a little.

Sibyl How?

Bob Well, like a referee helps in a boxing match. If you get in a clinch with them, I'll step right in and break it up.

Sibyl Then you're going to be quite busy!

Bob Don't go looking for a quarrel, sweetie. Play it cool, that's my advice. Don't put their backs up. If you do, they'll take it out on all of us. They're here to stay until this darned war's over. That's a fact we've got to live with, and we may as well face up to it. Has anyone gone down to meet them?

Sibyl Yes, I've sent the Seneschal down to the harbour and he's going to bring them straight up here.

Bob What—all of them? When I looked at that boat through my binoculars, it looked like they were packed together like sardines.

Sibyl There must be someone in command.

Bob Let's hope so.

Sibyl And I've been up to the school to reassure them all.

Bob How did you manage that?

Sibyl I told the children every German's not like Hitler necessarily.

Bob Right.

Sibyl So not to be frightened of them and treat them just like the ordinary tourists.

Bob Right.

Sibyl And don't keep saying "Right"!

Bob Why not? I'm paying you a compliment. You've done all the right things so far.

Sibyl I hope so.

Bob Course you have. You couldn't have done better. So relax.

Sibyl How can I, Bob?

Bob Why not? We've been expecting this since Dunkirk.

Sibyl I know. But now it's happened.

Bob Right. Sorry, sweetie, it slipped right out. Hey, it's coming out, I think. Sweetie—honey—come over here and help me.

Sibyl moves to the table

There—there—no, maybe not. Which one? This or that one?

Sibyl (*tapping a card*) That one.

Bob O.K. Be it on your head if it's the wrong one. Now what?

Sibyl (*tapping another card*) That one

Bob moves the card

Now that—no, that. Now that. And that.

Bob Well, what do you know! Well done, sweetie—I never could have done it without you. (*He begins collecting his cards*) Do you think there's time for one more?

Sibyl No, I don't. We must get ready for them.

Bob Ready for them! Put out drinks, you mean?

Sibyl No, I don't. You tidy up the cards and I'll pouff up the cushions.

Bob Listen to her! Pouff the cushions! What a woman you are!

Sibyl (*pouffing the cushions*) Put the cards away, Bob, and stop laughing at me.

Bob I'm not laughing at you, honey. I'm struck dumb with admiration for you.

Sibyl Dumb's not quite the right word, is it?

Bob (*putting the cards on the bookcase and replacing the table*) Pouffing up the cushions for a lot of bloody Germans who, for all you know, are going to hold you down and rape you.

Sibyl Over your dead body, I hope!

Bob I'm neutral, don't forget!

Sibyl (*abandoning the joking suddenly*) Oh, Bob, I'm frightened.

Bob sits with her on the firestool

Bob Take it easy, sweetie. I was only joking.

Sibyl I know, but we shouldn't joke about it—it might happen.

Bob Not while I'm around it won't.

Sibyl But they might shoot you.

Bob Shoot a United States' citizen? They wouldn't dare.

Sibyl I hope you're right.

Bob Of course I'm right. So relax. All Germans aren't like Hitler, as you just said. Try to remember that, honey, when you're dealing with them. Soldiers are just puppets, so it's no use blaming them—the guy responsible is the manipulator.

Sibyl What about the dreadful things they did in Poland?

Bob Wars are dreadful things, and dreadful things get done in them. But we're not in a war zone. We're demilitarized.

Sibyl They bombed Guernsey last week.

Bob Right. But that could have been a mistake.

Sibyl A mistake! Machine gunning our fishermen on their way home? You mustn't make excuses for them, Bob.

Bob Right. I'll wait and let them make their own.

Sibyl If they can think of any.

Bob Sibyl. (*He turns her round to face him*) Look me in the eye and tell me if you're really frightened.

Sibyl Yes, I am. I'm frightened for myself, and you for everyone on Sark—aren't you?

Bob No. I'm apprehensive, I admit. After all, who wouldn't be? Not frightened though. And nor are you. Those Germans walking up the road won't know what's hit them when they meet you. You will put them in their place and you will keep them in their place until the War's won— mark my words, you will.

Sibyl It's you who should be doing that. You're the Seigneur. (*She goes to ring the bell*)

Bob Right. But you're the boss. I'm just your husband. Who are you ringing for?

Sibyl Cecile.

Bob Why?

Sibyl To prepare her.

Bob That's right. You're all right now the bell's gone. You've come right out of your corner fighting. And you won't be back in it until Armistice Day.

Sibyl When will that be, Bob?

Bob One month if you go down. Five years if you hang on. More, maybe. But never worry. We'll see it through no matter how long it lasts.

Sibyl But what about the islanders? Those that are left?

Bob They'll see it through as well—if we do. So just be calm, and don't fly off the handle when you see that uniform. Remember they're Germans and its regulation issue!

Cecile enters, behind her in the doorway are Mr and Mrs Bishop and the Cowman

Cecile You rang, Madam?

Sibyl Yes, I did, Cecile. There'll be some Germans here at any minute.

Cecile Yes, Madam. So they tell me.

Sibyl Who?

Cecile The Seneschal. He saw their boat coming in.

Sibyl That's right. I've sent him down to the harbour and told him to bring them up here.

Cecile Yes, Madam.

Sibyl Don't be frightened of them, Cecile.

Cecile No, Madam.

Sibyl Come in, Mrs Bishop.

Mr and Mrs Bishop and the Cowman come into the room

Now listen to me. As I've just told Cecile—you mustn't be frightened.

Mrs Bishop No, Madam.

Sibyl All Germans aren't like Hitler.

All No, Madam.

Sibyl And if they're soldiers, they're likely to be well behaved.

Mrs Bishop They say they weren't—not in Poland, Madam.

Sibyl I know. But we aren't in a war zone. We're demilitarized.

Mrs Bishop Yes, Madam.

Sibyl So there's no need to be frightened. Treat them like you treat the ordinary tourists. I've just told the children to do that, and they're quite looking forward to it.

Mrs Bishop I'm not wanting to be raped, Madam.

Sibyl No, Mrs Bishop, I don't think any of us are, but perhaps you and I need not be concerned too much on that score. We're not as young as we were, are we?

Mrs Bishop No, Madam, that's the trouble.

She sounds regretful and they all laugh

Bob Talking of rape, Mrs Bishop, I hope you're not like the African who told her boss that she wouldn't go home through a certain wood because a girl had been raped there the night before. And her boss said, "Don't be silly, Agnes, why should anyone want to rape you?" And she said— "Waal, baas, ma trouble is that I rape very easily."

They all laugh

Sibyl All right, remember what I said. Now, go back to the farm and carry on as usual.

Chorus Yes, Madam, thank you, Madam, etc.

Mr and Mrs Bishop and the Cowman leave

Cecile moves to the door

Sibyl (*to Cecile, as she is about to follow the others*) Now, Cecile, when they get here, treat them just as you would any other guests.

Cecile Yes, Madam.

Sibyl Ask their names, then show them in here.

Cecile Yes, Madam.

Sibyl All right, Cecile, thank you.

Cecile exits

(*To Bob*) Where's *The House that Hitler Built* and *Sawdust Caesar*?
Bob In my study, I think.
Sibyl Get them, will you, Bob?
Bob What for? You are never going to read them to them, are you?
Sibyl No, of course not. Don't be silly. Hurry up, dear, they'll be here at any minute.
Bob Right.

Bob exits to the study

Sibyl stands contemplating the room. Then she moves two high-backed chairs to the window side of the dining-table, facing the room

Bob returns, carrying the books

Sibyl Thank you, darling.
Bob What's the idea of the two thrones?
Sibyl They're for you and me.
Bob We're not royal, honey.
Sibyl We're the equivalent on Sark. But that's not why I've done it. I got the idea from Mussolini. I read it in an article. Apparently that's what he does. He makes his visitors walk right from the door, right through the room, right up to his desk, and, by the time they've got there, they're so out of breath, Musso can do what he likes with them. (*During this speech she is deciding where to put the books, and finally places them, very prominently, on the little table by Bob's chair*)
Bob I guess his room's bigger than ours.
Sibyl Never mind that. We must do the best we can with what we've got.
Bob Right. What's the idea putting those there?
Sibyl To annoy them. And to see what sort of people they are. If they look at them and do nothing, it'll mean they're frightened of us. If they tell us to remove them, it'll mean they're petty-minded. And if they just ignore them maybe there's something to them.
Bob A barometer in covers—well I never.
Sibyl (*moving to the chairs*) Come and sit down, Bob. Which side do you prefer?
Bob I'm easy.
Sibyl Which side does the King sit when he opens Parliament?
Bob Don't ask me.
Sibyl On the right, I think. I'm sure he does.
Bob But you're the hereditary ruler.
Sibyl You're the Seigneur.
Bob Right, but you're still the boss.

Bob pulls out Sibyl's chair and she sits. He sits in the other one

Sibyl All right. (*She settles in*) All right?

Bob Yeah, I'm all right. But what about them?

Sibyl What about them?

Bob Aren't they going to sit down?

Sibyl Certainly not. Not to start with, anyway. Later on, if they're civil, I may consider it.

Bob (*laying a hand on her arm*) That's her—that's my Sibyl.

Sibyl What does that mean?

Bob It means that you've come out fighting, as I said you would. The Monstrous Regiment of Women!

Sibyl Bob!

Bob Don't get me wrong. I mean it as a compliment. Maybe the guy who wrote it didn't, but he was a man.

Sibyl Aren't you?

Bob Yes, but I'm broader-minded. (*Pause*) How long have we got to sit here?

Sibyl Till they come.

Bob Can I get my tobacco?

Sibyl From your study?

Bob No, the bookcase.

Sibyl If you hurry. (*She looks anxiously through the window*)

Bob (*getting up*) Thanks, Sarge! (*He goes to get his tobacco, and notices her anxious gaze through the window*)

Bob You remind me of the mother of the conchie at the Tribunal. I was told it in the Club the last time we were over on the mainland. Did I ever tell you?

Sibyl I expect so.

Bob Well, this conchie wouldn't budge. Whatever the Court said to him, he stuck his toes in, wouldn't go and fight at any price. Then finally the President, some peppery old colonel from my war, tried one last argument: "What would you do, young fellow, if a German soldier came here and attacked your mother?" he asked. And the conchie replied, "I'd lay three to one on Mum." (*He notices something through the window*) They're coming up the drive.

Sibyl How many are there?

Bob Two, that I can see.

Sibyl What? Officers or soldiers?

Bob They look pretty smart to me. Now watch your tongue. They could be tricky customers to deal with.

Sibyl We've done nothing wrong.

Bob So far.

There is a knock on the front door

Sibyl Come and sit down.

Bob Right.

Sibyl Oh, Bob, I'm really frightened now.

Bob No need to be. Just play it cool, and everything'll be O.K.

Cecile's voice is heard outside saying "Names, please?"

Should I put out my pipe?
Sibyl Certainly not. Smoke it in their faces. This is our home, not theirs.
Bob For the moment.
Sibyl Bob!
Bob Take it easy, honey. Keep your powder dry.

Cecile enters

Cecile Major Lanz and Dr Braun.
Sibyl Show them in, please, Cecile.
Cecile Will you come in, please.

Two German officers enter and give the Nazi salute. Bob attempts to rise politely, but is prevented by Sibyl

Braun Mr and Mrs Hathaway?
Bob That's right.
Braun This is Major Lanz. He will be Commandant on Sark. I am Dr Braun. The Major speaks no English. I interpret for him.
Sibyl I see.
Braun Mr Hathaway, you are the Seigneur of Sark?
Bob Right. But through my wife. She is the hereditary ruler, but our Constitution lays down that responsibility is shared between us equally.
Braun For governing the island?
Bob Right.
Sibyl But we are not dictators. We owe our allegiance to the King of England as our overlord. Kindly tell him that.
Braun (*to Lanz*) Mrs Hathaway sagt sie sei der erbliche Regierer aber unter der Constitution seilt sie die Verantwortung mit ihrem Mann. Sie erinnert uns daran, das sie dem Konig von England Treue geschworen haben.
Lanz Ich habe davon gehort.
Braun I have told him.
Sibyl Please also tell him that we are receiving you here at the Seigneurie because it is the custom on this island to receive all visitors here, no matter who they may be, and for no other reason.
Braun (*to Lanz*) Mrs Hathaway sagt das sie uns nor empfangt weil es auf der Insel Gebrauch ist alle Besucher in der Seigneurie zu empfangen wer sie auch sein mogen.
Lanz Ich freue mich das die Dame sich so korrekt benimmt.
Braun So . . .
Sibyl Good. Now, what is your business?
Braun The Channel Islands have been occupied by Germany. But you already know this.
Sibyl Yes, we heard you had arrived on Guernsey just before the telephones were cut.
Braun So. A proportion of the occupation force will naturally be stationed here on Sark. The soldiers have arrived with us this morning. They are

at the harbour now until the preparations have been made for billeting them. How many inhabitants remain here on the island?

Sibyl About five hundred. Only about fifty people were evacuated. Mostly English settlers.

Braun Why did you not leave yourselves, Mrs Hathaway?

Sibyl Because we thought it our duty to remain and guard the interests of our people—no matter what the consequences might be.

Braun I see. I have here the proclamation of the Commandant of all the German forces in the Channel Islands. (*He produces a poster from his briefcase*) And, in order to ensure that they are fully understood by all your islanders, you are required to place this poster in some prominent position.

Sibyl Show it to me, please.

Braun Certainly (*He hands it to her*)

Bob Where did you learn your English, Doctor?

Braun I studied tropical diseases in England for eight years.

Bob Bless my soul. A German posting's just like any other posting, is it?

Braun In what way?

Bob Well, in its eccentricity, I guess. You know, you won't find any tropical diseases in Guernsey and still less on Sark.

Braun You are not English?

Bob No, I'm an American.

Braun and Lanz exchange glances

Braun Then you are not my enemy.

Bob That's up to you.

Braun Your wife is English, though?

Sibyl I'm nothing of the kind. I am a Serquais. I am the elder daughter of the twentieth Seigneur of Sark. Kindly tell him that.

Braun (*to Lanz*) Herr Hathaway ist Amerikaner. Seine Frau ist eine geborene Serquais.

Lanz Richtig.

Sibyl Also tell him that Mr Hathaway is my second husband. My first husband died during an influenza epidemic after active service in the fourteen-eighteen war—in which Mr Hathaway also served as an air-pilot. And my son, by my first marriage, is now serving in the Royal Air Force.

Braun (*to Lanz*) Dies ist ihr sweiter Mann. Ihr erster Mann ist in der Epidemie nach dem Krieg neunzehn-vierzehn-achtzehn gestorben. Ihr Sohn aus der Ehe ist jetzt bei der englischen Luftwaffe. Herr Hathaway war Pilot im ersten Weltkrieg.

Lanz Ich verstehe.

Bob (*rising*) Now you know all about us. What about you?

Braun I am S.S., representing the civil administration of the occupation forces.

Bob I see. And will you be stationed here?

Braun No, I will be at headquarters in Guernsey.

Bob Right.

Sibyl Oh, Bob. You'd better look at this too.
Bob But I can't read German.
Sibyl It's in English as well. (*She hands the poster to him*)
Braun You read German?
Sibyl Badly.
Braun (*to Lanz*) Sie kann Deutsch lesen.
Lanz (*to Sybil*) Sie haben keine Angst?
Sibyl Gibt es einen Grund warum ich vor einem deutschen Officier Angst
haben sollte?
Lanz Uberhaupt keinen.
Bob What's all that about?
Sibyl He asked me if I were not afraid.
Bob And what did you say?
Sibyl I said was there any reason for me to be afraid of a German officer?
Bob And what did he say?
Sibyl None whatever. (*To Lanz*) I'm very glad to hear that.
Bob (*looking up from the poster*) So, my old rook rifle's got to go?
Sibyl Yes, Bob. You'd better go and get it.
Braun (*stopping him*) Not now. It will be collected later.

Bob stands by the fire, reading the poster. Braun collects his briefcase and prepares to go

Sibyl Why did you bomb Guernsey last week?
Braun It was a mistake. The British Government had not informed the
German Government that you had been demilitarized.
Sibyl Why should I believe that?
Braun You believe it or not, as you wish. But it is the truth.
Sibyl German pilots machine-gunned our fishermen on their way home.
That too is the truth.
Braun Very likely.
Sibyl Unarmed fishermen!
Braun Did Mr Hathaway not fire at anything suspicious from his aero-
plane in the nineteen-fourteen war?
Bob (*without looking up from the poster he is still reading*) You bet I did!
Sibyl And what is so suspicious about fishing boats?
Braun Our pilots no doubt thought that they were fishing on behalf of
those whom we then thought to be our enemies.
Sibyl We are still your enemies, Dr Braun, demilitarized or not.
Bob Well, this doesn't look too bad, all things considered. The curfew
won't affect us much on Sark. There's not a lot to do at night here, as
you may imagine. We're a little short on nightclubs. But I must say I
don't like this bit very much—"All sale of liquor forbidden—licensed
premises to be closed". Surely that can't be right?
Braun It is right, yes, Mr Hathaway. By order of the Commandant.
Bob But where am I going to get it?
Braun I'm afraid you will not get it.
Bob But the war may last for years.

Braun I think that is unlikely. We will finish it by Christmas. We will occupy your country——

Bob Oh no, not my country you won't, doc!

Braun I stand corrected. I mean England.

Bob And how do you propose to do that?

Braun By invading her, of course. How else?

Bob You're going to lose a lot of men.

Braun Perhaps a million.

Bob And that doesn't bother you?

Braun No. Not if it is necessary to do so.

Bob It'll be necessary, all right. The Channel's quite a formidable proposition, Doctor.

Braun We will overcome it.

Bob That's what Philip of Spain thought. And Bonaparte.

Braun William of Normandy, too.

Bob Harold had no navy.

Braun William had no aeroplanes.

Bob Nor did Harold, I guess.

During this exchange Major Lanz notices the books on the table. Braun also notices them and draws himself up

Braun Many of our soldiers buy the tweed material on Guernsey.

Bob Oh? Why?

Brain To make into suits of clothes when we arrive in London.

Bob You'll be lucky.

Sibyl You will never succeed in invading England, Dr Braun. Not in a thousand years.

Braun We will see, won't we, Mrs Hathaway?

Sibyl You will, indeed. Is there any further business?

Braun I ask. (*To Lanz*) Sie fragen, ob wir noch andere Anliegen haben.

Lanz Sagen sie ihnen, dass wir jetzt die Insel inspiezieren und entscheiden werden, wo wir unsere Manner einquatieren. Dann werde ich hicher zunickkommen.

Braun He say he will inspect the island to decide where he will billet his men, then return here to inform you what he wish to requisition.

Sibyl In that case, perhaps you will excuse my husband and myself. We have a lot of work to do. The island doesn't run itself, you know. I'll ring for my maid to see you out. (*She rings the bell*)

Braun You have hurt your foot, Mrs Hathaway?

Sibyl I was dropped by my nurse when I was a baby. It doesn't worry me.

Braun I see. (*To Bob*) And you will place this poster in a prominent position?

Bob O.K., honey?

Sibyl No.

Bob Sibyl . . .

Braun It is an order, Mrs Hathaway.

Sibyl Who from?

Braun The Commandant in Guernsey.
Sibyl Who is he?
Braun Herr Oberst von Schmettau.
Sibyl And he told you to tell me to put up this poster, personally?
Braun The poster must be put up in a prominent position on the island.
Bob Right. Then I've got a suggestion, Doctor. Take it with you now, and stick it anywhere you want to stick it.

Braun stiffens visibly

I suggest outside the store, or on the school house, or down at the harbour.

Cecile enters

Braun (*coldly*) Thank you, Mr Hathaway.
Sibyl Ah, Cecile, these officers are now leaving.
Cecile Yes, Madam.
Sibyl Will you show them out, please?
Cecile Yes, Madam.

The officers give a Nazi salute

This way, gentlemen.
Sibyl And Cecile . . .
Cecile Yes, Madam?
Sibyl Come back here immediately you've seen them off.
Cecile Yes, Madam.

Lanz, Dr Braun and Cecile exit

Sibyl She called them "gentlemen".
Bob Right.
Sibyl Well, she mustn't, and I'm going to tell her so.
Bob What's in a name? I guess the Major's O.K., but I didn't go for Dr Braun.
Sibyl Neither did I.
Bob And did you show it!
Sibyl What about you—saying that about the poster?
Bob Yeah—I shouldn't have. It doesn't do to put their backs up, but I just couldn't resist it.

Cecile enters

Cecile Yes, Madam?
Sibyl Cecile, those two men were officers, not gentlemen.
Cecile I thought it was the same thing, Madam.
Sibyl Not in their case.
Cecile I'm very sorry, Madam.
Sibyl That's all right, Cecile. You'll know another time.

Cecile exits

Bob Let's put the chairs back, honey. We look like we're in a dentist's waiting-room.

Sibyl They looked at the books, Bob.

Bob Yes, I saw them.

Sibyl And they didn't dare say anything. You were wonderful. What would I do without you? They won't take you away, will they?

Bob No—why should they?

Sibyl Because you're not Sark-born.

Bob No, of course not.

Sibyl He seemed very interested about you being an American.

Bob Well, it is an interesting nationality! I got away with it, you see. I told you I would.

Sibyl For the moment—Bob, if they took you away, I couldn't go on.

Bob Nonsense.

Sibyl No, I couldn't, Bob, I couldn't . . .

Bob Like a bet on it? I'll lay you three to one on! O.K., Mum?

the CURTAIN *falls*

PRELUDE TO SCENE 2

Here is the news and this is Alvar Lidell reading it.

During the night the Royal Air Force carried out their heaviest raid yet on German territory. Berlin, Bremen and Hamburg were the targets. The Germans, in their raids over Britain, lost nine of their bombers, and, in addition to this record total, two Messerschmitts have been destroyed since dawn.

The German Air Force last night paid its highest price of the war for night attacks on Britain when attempting their first large-scale raid for some time.

Last night, the moon being full and the weather very clear, the enemy, attempting his first large-scale raid for some months, attacked Mersey-side in force. On this occasion, however, the damage and casualties bore no relation to the scale of the attack, and very little was achieved beyond serious damage to a number of private houses. There were isolated incidents in other parts of the country. Nine enemy bombers are known to have been destroyed.

Since this communiqué was issued it has been made known that Royal Air Force night fighters . . .

SCENE 2

The same. Spring 1941

Sibyl is sitting at a table filling in forms. Bob is playing patience

Sibyl How many cows on the island, Bob?

Bob Around a hundred, I guess.

Sibyl I'll put a hundred and three. It looks better. Corn? Potatoes?

Bob Now look, sweetie, I'll fill those in later. It requires a very complex calculation to assess the weight of corn we harvest, less what we hide in the barn and grind ourselves when no-one's looking. Same with the potatoes.

Sibyl And how many rabbits?

Bob Well, I guess that figure varies quite considerably.

Sibyl It's no use putting that. They wouldn't understand about a rabbit's individuality. Besides its got to be a figure.

Bob Wild or tame?

Sibyl It doesn't say.

Bob Well, short of going down their holes to see who's pregnant and who isn't—it's pretty hard to come up with an accurate assessment.

Sibyl I'll put fifteen hundred.

Bob Why not? It's a good round figure. And, if they don't like it, we'll tell them to go down themselves and make a spot check.

Sibyl (*reading*) "Estimate of future revenue." How can we possibly answer that when we never know from day to day how many German troops are stationed on the island.

Bob We can't.

Sibyl Well, what shall I put?

Bob Think of a number, and then double it.

Sibyl Bob, you're being irresponsible.

Bob I'm not. I'm just working on the principle that a damn silly question deserves an equally damn silly answer. They'll learn.

Sibyl They've been here nearly a year and they haven't learnt yet.

Bob They're only the office boys, sweetie. You know, the civil servants. They sit behind their little desks in Guernsey wishing they were still on sewage in the Farterland. Still, the Army's learnt something.

Sibyl What?

Bob Well, Major Lanz has learnt a bit of English.

Sibyl And a lot of good its done him. Issuing that silly order about fishing.

Bob To be fair, that was the office boys too.

Sibyl I daresay. But he's a fool to have tried to enforce it. He's the laughing stock of the whole island.

Bob He did promise to refer it back to Guernsey. You've got to give him that.
Sibyl Two months ago. And nothing's happened yet.
Bob Oh, well. The military mind grinds slowly as a general rule.
Sibyl They're being bloody-minded, because the Blitz was a failure, and they couldn't have their tweed made up in Savile Row.
Bob Could be, but you can't tell them that.
Sibyl Oh, how I'd like to!
Bob Yes, I know you would, honey, but you mustn't.

A car is heard outside

Sibyl Who's that?
Bob (*looking out of the window*) Major Lanz.
Sibyl What does he want?
Bob Don't ask me. Maybe it's about the fishing.
Sibyl Or the wireless.
Bob Well, he's got no soot on him, so he hasn't come down the chimney and that's where I stuck the set last night. Maybe this is the moment for your daily resolution. Now, repeat after me please. Since all wireless sets were confiscated, I must not discuss the Blitz or any other piece of news. Right?

A knock is heard at the front door

Sibyl Since all wireless sets were confiscated, I must not discuss the Blitz or any other piece of news.
Bob Because they'll find out, if I do.
Sibyl ⎫
Bob ⎭ We only handed in one set instead of two (*Speaking together*)

Cecile enters

Cecile Major Lanz is here, Madam.
Sibyl What does he want?
Cecile To see Mr Hathaway.
Sibyl Well, show him in.
Cecile He wants to talk to Mr Hathaway alone, Madam.
Sibyl Nonsense. His English isn't good enough. Show him in.
Cecile Yes. Very good, Madam.

Cecile exits

Sibyl He thinks you're easier to deal with than I—because you're neutral.
Bob Well, that's certainly a point of view.
Sibyl It's the right one, too.

Cecile enters

Cecile Major Lanz, Madam.

Lanz enters. Cecile exits

Lanz Mrs Hathaway. Good morning, Mr Hathaway.
Bob Good morning, Major.
Sibyl Well, what is it you want?
Lanz I wish to speak to Mr Hathaway alone.
Sibyl Your English isn't good enough.
Lanz It is not bad, no?
Sibyl Is it about the fishing?
Lanz Nein.
Sibyl Have you heard from Guernsey yet?
Lanz Nein.
Sibyl You told them that it's no use fishing when the tide's wrong, did you?
Lanz Ja.
Sibyl Well then, what is it?
Lanz I wish to speak to Mr Hathaway alone.
Sybil There is nothing you can say to Mr Hathaway that you cannot also say to me.
Lanz I beg your pardon.
Sibyl Es gibt nichts——
Lanz (*interrupting*) Yes, I understand. But I do not agree. I have my orders that I speak with Mr Hathaway alone.
Sibyl Who from?
Lanz Herr Oberst von Schmettau.
Bob He's not going to budge, honey. Leave him with me and I'll tell you later. (*To Lanz*) Will that be in order?
Lanz Yes, most certainly.
Sibyl Oh, very well. I'll go into the garden. But it does seem to me extraordinarily childish.

Sibyl exits to the garden

Bob Have a seat?
Lanz No, thank you. Mr Hathaway, it is bad news.
Bob So, I'm due for deportation, eh?
Lanz No, it is not that.
Bob Well, what is it then?
Lanz Your step-son—he has been killed.
Bob What—Buster?
Lanz Flight-Lieutenant Beaumont.
Bob That's right. Oh God. (*He sits down*)
Lanz I am sorry.
Bob Was he on a flying mission?
Lanz I do not know.
Bob Poor old Buster.
Lanz I am sorry if I upset Mrs Hathaway, but I was told to give the news to you.

Bob Quite right. Most thoughtful of whoever told you.
Lanz The Herr Commandant.
Bob Well, thank him for me, will you?
Lanz There is no need. He comes here to offer his condolences in person.
Bob When?
Lanz He is inspecting the defences of the island now.
Bob I see. I wonder how he got the news?
Lanz I have not been told.
Bob (*rising*) Well, thank you, Major Lanz. I'm most grateful to you.
Lanz Thank you, Mr Hathaway.

Lanz exits

Bob goes to the bookcase for his pouch and walks to the fireplace. There is the sound of a car leaving

Sibyl enters from the garden

Sibyl Well, what did he want?
Bob (*moving to her*) Bad news, darling. Very bad news. About Buster.
Sibyl He's dead?
Bob Yes, honey. I'm afraid so. Sit down, honey. Sit down. (*He helps her to a chair*) I know, I know, I know. Would you like a little brandy?

Sibyl indicates "no"

Why not? I know I would.
Sibyl All right, if you're going to.
Bob Right. I'll go and get it. (*He goes to the door and turns*) Sure you're all right?
Sibyl Yes, Bob.
Bob That's my Sibyl.

Bob exits to the study

Sibyl remains seated

Bob returns with two glasses and a decanter of brandy on a tray. He puts it on a table, and Sibyl comes over

Sibyl Was he flying, Bob?
Bob Lanz didn't know. I would imagine so. Here, sweetie. (*He hands her a brandy*)
Sibyl How did they find out? (*She sits*)
Bob Don't ask me. All I know is Major Lanz was told to tell me and not you. (*He takes his glass and goes to a chair*)
Sibyl Who by?
Bob Von Schmettau.
Sibyl (*not concentrating*) Who's he?

Bob He's the Commandant on Guernsey.
Sibyl Oh yes, of course.
Bob He's on his way here.
Sibyl I won't see him.
Bob Well, if that's what you want, sweetie. But he's been most thoughtful.
And he may know more about the circumstances.
Sibyl You can see him, Bob, can't you?
Bob Yes, of course I will. Why don't you go and have a lie down? Finish
up your brandy first.
Sibyl I can't. It's too strong.
Bob Please, dear. It'll do you good.
Sibyl Did Major Lanz know when it happened?
Bob No. I guess the Commandant'll tell us all that.
Sibyl Trust a German to barge in at a time like this.
Bob Don't get bitter, honey. It won't help.

There is a knock at the front door

That'll be him, I guess. You'd better get moving.
Sibyl No, I'm going to stay. I don't want him to think that I can't take it.
Bob Good girl.

Cecile enters

Cecile Colonel Count von Schmettau, Madam.
Sibyl Show him in, Cecile.
Cecile Will you come in, please.

Von Schmettau enters. Cecile exits

Bob I'm Bob Hathaway.
Von Schmettau Rudolph von Schmettau.
Bob And this is my wife.

Von Schmettau bows. Sibyl stares ahead

Von Schmettau I am sorry our first meeting should be on this sad occasion.
May I offer my sincere condolences to both of you.
Bob Thank you. That's very kind of you.
Von Schmettau I understand your feelings, Mrs Hathaway, believe me, if
you look upon my presence as an unforgivable intrusion. None the less,
I thought it right to come. My heartfelt sympathy extends to all the
mothers of all nations who grieve in the same way for their sons. I
hope that we may meet again in less unhappy circumstances. (*He clicks
his heels*)
Sibyl Please, don't go. Forgive my rudeness. Won't you sit down?

Von Schmettau looks at Bob, who indicates a chair

Von Schmettau Thank you. (*He sits*)
Bob Would you care for some brandy?

Von Schmettau No, you must not tempt me. I have work to do.

Sibyl Thank you for what you have just said.

Von Schmettau I meant it, Mrs Hathaway.

Sibyl I know you did. And I appreciate it. How did you find out about my son?

Von Schmettau I understand a relative of yours informed the United States Embassy in London. From there the message was passed to Berlin, then on to me, with a request that I should see that you were informed.

Sibyl Do you know how . . .?

Von Schmettau It appears your son was on leave, in an hotel in Liverpool. And—there was a bombing-raid . . .

Bob Poor old Buster.

Sibyl And the date?

Von Schmettau The twenty-ninth.

Sibyl Bob, what's today?

Bob Wednesday, the thirty-first

Sibyl Monday. It must have been on Monday.

Von Schmettau I regret that I can tell you no more. (*He gets up and moves to the door*)

Sibyl (*changing the subject in order to avoid breaking down, a situation which von Schmettau appreciates at once*) What about our fishing hours?

Von Schmettau Your fishing hours?

Sibyl Don't you know about it?

Von Schmettau Know what?

Sibyl About the control.

Von Schmettau No, I don't think so. Please tell me.

Sibyl Major Lanz said he'd raised the subject with you.

Von Schmettau With me?

Sibyl With your headquarters in Guernsey.

Sibyl moves to her table and picks up some papers. Von Schmettau follows her

Von Schmettau Ah! Yes. Many things reach my headquarters. But they do not always reach me. Not unless they are of great importance.

Sibyl This is vitally important.

Von Schmettau My apologies. What is the difficulty?

Sibyl Fishing hours—from ten a.m. to three p.m.

Von Schmettau Five hours. Is that not reasonable?

Sibyl It's a waste of time. You can't fish when the tide's not right.

Von Schmettau I see. Then what do you suggest I do?

Sibyl Revoke the order. It's all nonsense. Let our fishermen fish when they want to. They know more about it than you. They don't tell you how to run your army, do they?

Von Schmettau Not if they are sensible.

Sibyl Well, why can't you be sensible as well?

Von Schmettau I stand corrected. Very well, I will see what can be done.

Sibyl Thank you.

Von Schmettau Have you any further complaints?

Sibyl Oh yes, plenty. Look at this form: an estimate of future revenue.

Von Schmettau Can you not make one?

Sibyl As we never know from day to day how many of your troops are on the island, and, as you make us pay for their maintenance, it's quite impossible to make an estimate.

Von Schmettau Again I offer my apologies. Very well, I will try to keep the numbers constant, provided you behave yourselves. Is that a bargain, Mrs Hathaway?

Sibyl Yes.

Von Schmettau Well—in that case . . .

Sibyl Just look at this stupid form. The whole thing's absurd.

Von Schmettau You have my sympathy, I must confess. It is a formidable document.

Sibyl Look at question seven. "Estimate of rabbit population!"

Von Schmettau Rabbits?

Sibyl Kaninchen.

Von Schmettau Rabbits.

Sibyl That's what I said.

Von Schmettau (*putting the forms back on the table*) In self-defence I must point out that this is not my responsibility. Rabbits are a civil matter.

Sibyl But you're the Commander-in-Chief, aren't you?

Von Schmettau Indeed.

Sibyl Well then, you can tell them not to be so ridiculous.

Von Schmettau In theory, yes. But in practice, no. A rebuke from the military is not always well received by the bureaucracy.

Sibyl You mean the S.S. They aren't interested in rabbits, surely?

Von Schmettau It is their function to be interested in everything, Mrs Hathaway.

Sibyl studies the form and moves to sit down at the table

Bob You'd be a regular—would that be right, Colonel?

Von Schmettau Yes. I joined the army many years ago. Too long ago for comfort. When I was seventeen to be exact. The Cavalry.

Bob So you were in my war too—well, I can see you were. I was a pilot.

Von Schmettau So I understand.

Bob So you've been checking up on me?

Von Schmettau Naturally.

Bob Yes. You're lucky to have got this job, I reckon. One assumes you don't like Mr Hitler very much.

Von Schmettau The Fuhrer is the leader of my country. Democratically elected.

Bob Right. Don't get me wrong. I didn't mean to give offence. And if I've given it, I'm sorry. All I thought was maybe an old war-horse like you might have had enough of fighting. I know I have.

Von Schmettau It is my profession.

Bob O.K. Then why take this job, if you feel that way?

Von Schmettau Because I am unfit.

Bob I see.

Von Schmettau I was gassed on the Western Front in nineteen-eighteen. Now I have only one lung.

Bob Oh, I'm sorry.

Von Schmettau It was a long time ago. (*He turns to the seated Sibyl*) I have to go now, Mrs Hathaway.

Sibyl It was good of you to come, Colonel. (*Rising*) I'll ring for my maid.

Von Schmettau It has been a pleasure meeting you. (*To Bob*) And you, sir.

Bob Thank you. Come again when you're over this way.

Von Schmettau It will be a pleasure.

Cecile enters

I will see what can be done about the fishing hours, Mrs Hathaway.

Sibyl I should be very grateful.

Von Schmettau But I cannot promise to do much about your rabbit population.

Sibyl Never mind about that.

Bob Just so long as you persuade them to accept our estimate.

Von Schmettau I shall do what I can.

Von Schmettau and Cecile exit

Bob Well, well, Not bad. Not bad at all.

Sibyl That makes it worse. War's only tolerable if you hate your enemies. If they're nice, it's unendurable.

Bob They're not all nice. Not by a long chalk, honey.

Sibyl I wish none of them were.

Bob (*moving to the table*) Sweetie, where's the *Almanac de Gotha*?

Sibyl In the bookcase, I think.

Bob I'd like to check up on this von Schmettau. After all, he checked up on me. (*He finds the book on the shelf and brings it to the table*) And he didn't like what I said about Mr Hitler much!

Sibyl Did you expect him to?

Bob No. It was what my French friends call a *ballon d'essai*.

Sibyl What did it prove?

Bob What I thought it would. That he's an anti-Nazi.

Sibyl How do you work that out?

Bob Well, from his reaction. If he'd been pro-Nazi he'd have left out that excuse about Hitler being democratically elected. Nazis don't waste their time on things like that! (*Reading from the almanac*) Von Schmettau, Rudolph. Third son of Colonel Count von Schmettau and Hermine von Rundstedt. Well, what do you know! She'll be the sister of von Runstedt the Field Marshal!

Sibyl He's not anti-Nazi, is he?

Bob Time will show.

Sibyl Monday, he said, didn't he?

Bob Yes.

Sibyl What's today, Bob?

Bob Wednesday.

Sibyl Perhaps the funeral's today.

Bob Right.

Sibyl Or tomorrow. Which do you think, Bob?

Bob I really couldn't say, sweetie.

Sibyl Well, let's imagine it's today, and we'll sit out in the garden this afternoon and think about him. That's all we can do, really, isn't it?

She starts to move to the study door

Bob I guess so.

Sibyl Till the war's over. Then we can go to Liverpool and see his grave. The trains are quite good. We went up once for the National, do you remember?

Sibyl exits and closes the study door after her

the CURTAIN *falls*

PRELUDE TO SCENE 3

Here is the news and this is Alvar Lidell reading it.

The three fighting services have carried out another small night raid, details are not yet available. Our bombers have attacked aerodromes in the Low Countries, and again mined enemy waters.

The gap between the British First and Eighth Armies is narrowing. The Eighth Army was within seventy miles of Benghazi yesterday. Allied air-borne troops have captured a vital airfield in Tunisia, in one of the biggest parachute operations of the war. The Americans have bombed the airfield near Bizerta.

Home-based Flying Fortresses and Liberators have attacked Germany's Atlantic U-boat bases again. Today they raided Lorient and La Pallice. A combined operation was carried out in the early hours . . .

SCENE 3

The same. Autumn 1942.

Bob and Sibyl are at breakfast. Muller, a young German soldier, stands on guard by the door. Cecile is sitting on a chair in the background. A German soldier is seen walking past the window

Soldier (*off*) Haben sie die Stalle durchsucht?
Second Soldier (*off*) Jawohl, Hans.
Sibyl Have some more coffee, Bob?
Bob No, thank you.
Sibyl You'd better. It's the last cup you'll get till the war's over. We've run out.
Bob (*passing his cup*) Thanks. What about tomorrow?
Sibyl You'd better ask Cecile. She thought of it.
Cecile Sugar beet, barley and parsnips, sir.
Bob I can't wait to try that!
Sibyl It's not too bad. We didn't mind it too much when we tried it, did we, Cecile?
Cecile No, Madam.
Lanz (*off*) Sie drei durchsuchen das obere stockwerk. Die anderen durchsuchen die Stalle und alle Hofgebaude. Beeilen sie sich.
Sibyl They're going to search upstairs now, Bob.
Bob Good luck to them.
Sibyl What are they looking for?
Bob Don't ask me. (*Pointing at Muller*) Ask him.
Sibyl They've been here since six. It's after nine now . . .
Bob I know, sweetie, I know.
Sibyl You look tired, Bob.
Bob I am tired, honey. I never got off properly after all those bangs last night,
Sibyl Did you hear the explosions too, Cecile?
Cecile Yes, Madam. Just after midnight.
Sibyl Yes, that's right. So did we. Some very loud ones—then some less loud. Like machine-gun fire or rifles.
Cecile Yes, that's right, Madam.
Sibyl Do you think there's been a mutiny, Bob?
Bob (*looking at Muller*) Doesn't look that way.
Sibyl (*to Muller*) Did you hear the bangs last night?
Muller Ja.
Sibyl What was it? A bombardment from the sea—or a plane being shot down?
Muller I do not know.

Bob Or a raid perhaps?

Muller I do not know.

Bob I guess it was the rabbits setting off the trip-wires in the minefields. (*Getting up*) Well, I'd like to pay a visit somewhere.

Sibyl He won't let you.

Bob He'd better, if he doesn't want an accident. (*To Muller*) Hey, soldier—watch me. (*He pantomimes pulling the plug*) Get it?

Muller You are wishing for the toilet?

Bob Bless my soul, the lad's a linguist! (*To Muller*) That's right.

Muller Where is it, please?

Bob Just across the hall. (*He opens the door*) Through that door right there, see? (*Pointing*)

Muller Wait here, please.

Muller exits

Bob I guess he's gone to see if I can dive down the pan. (*He looks up*)

Sibyl (*in a low voice*) They'll find the wireless in the box-room.

Bob No, they won't. I stuck it up the chimney when the bangs woke me up last night.

Sibyl Oh, good.

Muller returns

Muller You may go. But do not close the door. And I leave this door open.

Bob O.K. Please yourself. (*He walks to the door, lighting his pipe*)

Sibyl Now, Bob, be careful with those matches. We're nearly out of them.

Bob exits

Sibyl sits in an armchair

I hope there weren't any casualties last night—in spite of all the shooting. Did it wake you up? I should imagine not as you're young. How old are you—sixteen?

Muller I seventeen.

Sibyl That's very young to be a soldier, isn't it? What's your name?

Muller Wilhelm Muller.

Sibyl And where do you come from?

Muller Munchen.

Sibyl That's a lovely town.

Muller I like it—ja.

Sibyl Your parents live there, do they?

Muller Ja.

Sibyl How many of you are there?

Muller I have two brother—two sister.

Sibyl And you're the youngest?
Muller No. I am the oldest.
Sibyl Then your parents must be quite young.
Muller Ja. My father he is forty, and my mother she is thirty-five.
Sibyl Is your father a soldier, too?
Muller Nein. He is a train driver. (*He looks round*) You like to see them?
  Here, I have a picture.
Sibyl Oh yes. Very much. (*She rises and goes to him*)

Muller takes a photo from his pocket, then looks into the hall

  You needn't worry about my husband. He'll be there for some time.

Muller gives her the photo

  Thank you. Father—mother—you . . .
Muller Ja.
Sibyl Next brother—elder sister—younger sister—youngest brother
Muller Correct.
Sibyl And who's this?
Muller She my fiancée.
Sibyl Oh, and what's her name?
Muller Ilse.
Sibyl She's very pretty.
Muller Dankeschön.
Sibyl You're a very lucky young man.
Muller Danke.
Sibyl Look, Cecile—oh, may I?
Muller Please.

Sibyl hands the photo to Cecile. Muller moves over to Cecile

Muller This Ilse.
Cecile Oh, yes. Very nice.

Major Lanz is heard outside. Muller snatches back the picture and stands guard again. Cecile goes back to her chair

  Lanz enters

Sibyl Well, Major Lanz, did you find anything?
Lanz (*ignoring her*) Wo ist Herr Hathaway?
Muller Er musste austreten.

  Lanz exits

Lanz (*off*) Mr Hathaway?
Bob (*off*) Yeah. What's the matter?
Lanz (*off*) I make sure you are there.
Bob (*off*) I'm here all right. I'll be out in a brace of shakes if you don't
  rush me. O.K.?

Lanz (*entering*) Warten sie im Flur.

Lanz enters. Muller exits

We find nothing, Mrs Hathaway.
Sibyl What did you expect to find?
Lanz We have to make the search in case the raiding party have left any
of their number on the island.
Sibyl What sort of raid was it?
Lanz A Commando raid.
Sibyl Bravo!

Bob enters

Bob Well, what did you find, Major? A battalion of guardsmen?
Lanz We find nothing, Mr Hathaway.
Bob Well, what did you expect?
Sibyl That was a Commando raid last night, Bob.
Bob Great!
Lanz Two English bodies washed up on the beach—and one German.
They tied our soldiers when they are taken prisoner, and shoot one of
them when he tried to escape. This is not war, it is murder.
Sibyl There's no difference, Major Lanz.
Lanz That is not true. Our army fights according to the military code. On
that we pride ourselves.
Bob In Poland?
Lanz What you hear of Poland, Mr Hathaway, was propaganda.
Bob That's your story, naturally.
Lanz It is the truth.
Bob Were you there?
Lanz No.
Bob Then how in hell do you know if it's true or not?
Lanz Because I know the German army.
Bob Well look—let me tell you something, Major. There's a lot of guys
around these days in German uniform in Poland, France and elsewhere,
who don't give that—(*he clicks his fingers*)—for your precious military
code. Do you admit that?
Lanz I am not responsible for them.
Bob You do admit it then. O.K. Let's leave it at that.
Lanz That does not excuse what your Commandos did last night.
Bob Oh no—not mine. I'm an American and let's leave that at that—O.K.,
Major?
Soldier (*off*) Derchsuchen Sie die Hofgebaude.
Second Soldier (*off*) Ja.

Lanz moves to the window to look out

Sibyl Major Lanz, I'm going into the garden. I'm not going far. I want to
get some flowers from the border by the front door.

Lanz Muller, Geleiten sie Frau Hathaway in den Garten. Aber passen sie auf.
Muller (*off*) Ja, Herr Major.
Lanz The guard will go with you.
Sibyl What about Cecile? She can't just sit here all the morning. She's got the housework to do.
Lanz She may do that.
Sibyl Thank you. Come along, Cecile.

Sibyl exits. Cecile puts back the chair from the table, picks up the breakfast tray, and follows Sibyl out

Lanz Mr Hathaway, the school must be evacuated.
Bob The school—why?
Lanz We need it for our men.
Bob Instruction in the military code?
Lanz For billets. And not only the school. Other houses in the centre of the island.
Bob Getting windy, are we?
Lanz Windy?
Bob Nervy.
Lanz It is necessary. The coastline is too dangerous. Besides the cliff tops are to be mined.
Bob You are getting nervy.
Lanz It is a precaution.
Bob Why didn't you tell my wife this?
Lanz You are the Seigneur, not your wife.
Bob That's not the reason, Major.
Lanz I find men are easier to deal with. They do not confuse the matter.
Bob My wife's not confused—far from it.
Lanz I did not say that. I said that matters were confused.
Bob Right. Then I stand corrected.
Lanz You will see these houses are evacuated?
Bob Which?
Lanz I have the list here. (*He hands a list to Bob*)
Bob Oh God—look here, Major, we can't have this. Major Brownrigg's seventy-five years old and his wife is even older.
Lanz I am sorry.
Bob And the Greys are not exactly in their first youth. Do you really have to do this?
Lanz Yes, it is an order.
Bob Who from?
Lanz The Herr Commandant.
Bob Well, I'm not going to tell them to obey it, Major. In fact, if I get the opportunity I'll tell them not to.
Lanz That would be unwise.
Bob Unwise or not, that's what I . . .

Sibyl enters, carrying a basket of chrysanthemums, scissors and string.
She goes over to the table

Sibyl—the Major says the Brownriggs and the Greys and all these others
have to be evacuated.
Sibyl Evacuated? Where to?
Bob Other people's houses, I guess—and the school.
Sibyl The school—whatever for?
Bob Because he's moving his troops inland.
Lanz After the Commando raid last night, the cliff tops are to be mined
and all German personnel moved into the centre of the island.
Sibyl So, you've started to retreat?

There is a knock on the front door

Whose stupid idea is this, Major Lanz?
Lanz It is an order from the High Command in Berlin.
Bob He wants us to back him up and tell them that they've got to go.
Sibyl On no account. On no account whatever, Major Lanz. If I tell them
anything at all, it'll be to stay where they are.
Bob That's what I said.
Lanz In that case they will be removed by force.

Von Schmettau enters

Lanz stands to attention

Sibyl What nonsense is this, Colonel?
Von Schmettau Nonsense? I know of no nonsense. I know only of the
cowardly raid last night.
Sibyl Whatever else it was, it was not cowardly.
Von Schmettau No? To tie up prisoners and then to shoot them when they
are attempting to escape?
Sibyl They shot one.
Von Schmettau Is not one enough? Or are you not content until there is
mass-murder?
Sibyl You shot two of our men.
Von Schmettau They were free.
Sibyl They're not free now. (*Pause*) We didn't start this war, Colonel, you
did—or rather your Fuhrer. So you mustn't blame us when we hit back.
You've no right to be in Sark or Guernsey or in any of the Channel
Islands—or in Poland, come to that, or Belgium or the Netherlands,
or France, or Africa. No-one invited you. You came. Now you must
take what's coming to you, and, make no mistake about it, it is coming—
slowly but inevitably, and your despicable little Fuhrer will be defeated
and your precious German army beaten.
Von Schmettau Do not speak like that.
Sibyl I'll speak exactly as I like!
Von Schmettau Then I will put you under arrest unless you apologize. At
once, please.

Sibyl Never.

Von Schmettau I insist. I give you just one minute.

Sibyl continues arranging her flowers, and does not answer

Bob You'd better do what he wants, honey.

Sibyl No, Bob.

Bob Come on, sweetie. After all you did insult him. You wouldn't like it if he said the same about the British army, would you?

Sibyl He just did.

Bob No, he didn't. All he said was that the boys shouldn't have tied up their prisoners last night. And, let's face it, it's a point of view. Backed up by the Geneva Convention, what's more. (*Pause*) Please, honey— he's not bluffing. He means what he says.

Sibyl (*after a pause*) I'm sorry.

Von Schmettau Thank you. Now it is forgotten. Major Lanz, you have informed this lady and her husband that some houses and the school must be evacuated?

Lanz Ja, Herr Oberst.

Von Schmettau (*to Sibyl*) You will co-operate?

Bob Look, Colonel—couldn't we——

Sibyl No. And neither will my husband.

Von Schmettau (*to Bob*) You mean this?

Bob I guess so.

Von Schmettau But surely you do not wish that they should be evicted by force? Because that is what will be done.

Sibyl You can't do that.

Von Schmettau Mrs Hathaway, it is an order from the High Command. I ask for your co-operation so that an unpleasant task may be performed as painlessly as possible. (*To Lanz*) Major Lanz, you will see that these houses and the school are cleared by midday.

Lanz Herr Commandant.

Lanz salutes and exits

Sibyl Oh, go with him, Bob, and tell them we did everything we could to stop it. But we couldn't.

Bob Right.

Bob follows Lanz out

Von Schmettau Now it is my turn to apologize.

Sibyl And so you should.

Von Schmettau Major Lanz heard you insult the Fuhrer, and I had no alternative but to demand an apology. I have every reason to believe that Major Lanz admires the Fuhrer greatly—as we all do.

Sibyl We're alone now, Colonel.

Von Schmettau As we all do, Mrs Hathaway.

Sibyl Yes, Colonel. I heard you the first time.

Von Schmettau Those flowers are very pretty.

Sibyl I want to put them on our soldiers' graves. Do you know when they will be buried?

Von Schmettau This afternoon, I believe.

Sibyl Do you know who they were?

Von Schmettau No. All identity marks were removed, or washed away perhaps. What is so regrettable about last night's raid, Mrs Hathaway, will be its quite inevitable aftermath.

Sibyl What does that mean?

Von Schmettau A tightening up of security. More soldiers stationed on Sark, and, in consequence, less food to be distributed among your people. Ultimately deportations.

Sibyl Clear the island, you mean?

Von Schmettau I hope that will not be necessary.

Sibyl What then?

Von Schmettau It is more than likely that the High Command will react strongly to last night's raid. They will then be forced to put in operation their contingency plans.

Sibyl Which are?

Von Schmettau To deport all those from your island who are not Sark born.

Sibyl That includes my husband?

Von Schmettau That is so. But if you were to write a letter to the Guernsey newspaper, stating that in your opinion any further raids on Sark would do incalculable harm—it is possible . . .

Sibyl Never! A German controlled paper—never!

Von Schmettau That could be to your advantage. We could see that what you wrote reached England.

Sibyl Never! I welcome these raids, Colonel—I welcome them!

Von Schmettau Very well, but remember what the consequences of them will inevitably be. And I have to say this, Mrs Hathaway, in spite of my apology, it was not right to tie the prisoners up.

Sibyl What's the use of making rules in war—the whole thing's bestial.

Von Schmettau Some decency should be preserved if possible.

Sibyl Like bombing little children in an air-raid?

Von Schmettau There will always be accidents.

Sibyl I doubt if Marshal Goering would be very pleased if he heard you refer to his raids on London as accidents.

Von Schmettau London is your capital city. It is a military objective.

Sibyl Nonsense.

Von Schmettau No, it is not nonsense. London is your seat of Government. The centre of administration of the war. If London goes, then Britain is defeated.

Sibyl But it didn't, did it?

Von Schmettau Nonetheless, it is a military target.

Sibyl So is Berlin.

Von Schmettau And Churchill has bombed it.

Sibyl Has he?

Von Schmettau Not to the same extent, of course.

Sibyl Of course.

Von Schmettau That is because he lacks the necessary strength. But once he possesses sufficient planes to do so on the same scale, he will do it.

Sibyl You don't really believe that. We're not that kind of people.

Von Schmettau There are no two kinds of people in war, Mrs Hathaway. One does what one must.

Sibyl Not bombing defenceless civilians.

Von Schmettau Even that.

Sibyl We'll never bomb Berlin as you bombed London.

Von Schmettau You will be proved wrong. I wish that you would not be, but you will be proved wrong. I will make a wager with you.

Sibyl What?

Von Schmettau Five hundred marks.

Sibyl Done. I want to put an inscription on the flowers. I assume you will allow me to do this?

Von Schmettau Certainly. If it is not subversive.

She writes on a card, and then hands it to him

Sibyl How will that do?

Von Schmettau (*reading aloud*) "They died that we might be free." But this is subversive, Mrs Hathaway.

Sibyl Not from my point of view.

Von Schmettau That is true. But you must not expect me to permit this.

Sibyl I do.

Von Schmettau Why so?

Sibyl Because you're an officer and a gentleman.

Von Schmettau There is no room for gentlemen in wartime, Mrs Hathaway. Or any other time perhaps, soon.

Sibyl That will be a pity.

Von Schmettau These flowers—they will be placed in the grave?

Sibyl Yes.

Von Schmettau Dropped on the coffins and then covered over?

Sibyl Yes, if that's what you want.

Von Schmettau I would prefer it to leaving them to wither and die on the surface. Very well, you may use that inscription on one condition.

Sibyl What?

Von Schmettau That you tear this up. (*He holds out the card*) Now.

Sibyl hesitates

Do as I say.

Sibyl tears up the card

Put it in the basket.

Sibyl puts the card in the wastepaper-basket

Good. Now—write it again.

Sibyl turns to the desk

But not until after I am gone.

Sibyl stops

And then, if there should be any objections I can say, with a clear conscience, that I have not seen it!

Von Schmettau turns and exits

the CURTAIN *falls*

PRELUDE TO SCENE 4

Here is the news and this is Alvar Lidell reading it.

The Russians have announced the final liquidation of the encircled German forces at Stalingrad. Yesterday the surviving enemy troops north of the city were forced to surrender and their Commander, General Strecker, was taken prisoner with seven other German Generals.

Our bombers were out over Germany last night. There's no important news from the other war fronts. Some more details have been given about Mr Churchill's visit to Cyprus.

It is quiet in Stalingrad today, for the first time for many months. The city yesterday devoured the last of the German hordes whom Hitler sent to capture it, to keep his promise and to bolster his prestige.

Altogether, during the fighting from the tenth of January up to yesterday . . .

SCENE 4

The same. Winter 1943

Sibyl is warming a pair of gloves by the fire. Bob is standing in the middle of the room wearing an overcoat and scarf. Muller is standing by the door

Bob Well, this is it, I guess.

Sibyl gives him the gloves

Thanks, sweetie.

Sibyl (*to Muller*) Can't we be alone for just a minute? Please? Go out into the hall and shut the door just for a moment.

Muller hesitates

Please.

Muller exits

Bob, what did you do with the letters the Brownriggs gave us?

Bob In the rabbit hutch, under the straw.

Sibyl Who were they to?

Bob Their friends in England.

Sibyl What was in them?

Bob Don't ask me.

Sibyl Why did they leave them here?

Bob I guess they thought they might not come back.

Sibyl Oh, Bob.

Bob I'll be O.K., sweetie. I'm tough. I'll survive a prison camp. They're both over seventy. In fact I wouldn't be surprised if Gwen's not pushing eighty. Deporting an old couple like that! It's inhuman!

Muller returns

Sibyl Darling.

Bob and Sybil embrace

Bob Well, look after yourself, honey.

Sibyl You too, Bob.

Bob (*picking up his hold-all*) Be seeing you ...

Sibyl Are you sure you've got everything?

Bob Yeah. Everything's not much these days, thank God.

Sibyl (*going through the hold-all*) Have you got those two shirts Cecile washed?

Bob Yeah—the two tailless wonders.
Sibyl Tailless? Did she burn them with the iron?
Bob No—you made me hankies out of them—remember?
Sibyl Oh yes. And the socks I darned?
Bob I'm wearing them.
Sibyl I darned two pairs.
Bob Yes—with red wool, too.
Sibyl It's all there was.
Bob I know. They're in. And my pyjamas. And my slacks and underpants.
  Two cardigans. Don't worry, honey. All present and correct.
Sibyl Your washing things?
Bob Yeah. Toothbrushes—two. One blue, one red in reserve.
Sibyl And your razor?
Bob Yeah. And blades—if they'll let me keep them. (*He turns to Muller*)
  O.K., son. Let's get going, or I'll miss that boat.
Sibyl I'm coming with you, Bob.
Bob No, honey. We agreed you wouldn't, last night.
Sibyl But I want to.
Bob No, I'd rather stick to schedule. We decided we'd say good-bye here
  and remember it that way, instead of on the quay among a lot of
  screaming Huns and seagulls.

They embrace once more

  Good-bye, honey. I'll write as soon as I reach my final destination.
Sibyl I'll never get it.
Bob Why not? (*He indicates Muller*) He gets his from his fiancée—don't
  you?
Muller Ja. One each week.
Bob There you are. The post works better now than it did in peacetime.
  Be seeing you.

Bob makes a "V" sign and exits to the hall with Muller

Sibyl goes over to the window to watch him go

Bob (*off*) Good-bye, Cecile.
Cecile (*off*) Good-bye, Mr Hathaway.
Bob (*off*) Look after yourself.
Cecile (*off*) Yes, Sir.
Bob (*off*) Look after my wife, too, won't you?
Cecile (*off*) Yes, Sir.
Bob (*off*) Sure, I know you will. You're a great girl, Cecile.

*Suddenly there is a lot of noise in the hall. Orders are barked in German and
English*

*Lanz and Muller enter: Muller is carrying Bob's hold-all. At a sign from
Lanz he puts it on a chair.*

Braun enters and begins tossing out the contents of the hold-all. A protesting Bob brings up the rear

Sibyl stands amazed

Bob Hey, what's going on?

Braun pockets the razor blades and signs to Muller to repack the hold-all

Braun (*to Muller*) Haben sie die sechen auf.

Muller repacks the hold-all

(*To Bob*) You have some letters in your pocket?
Bob Letters? Who the hell from?
Braun Major Brownrigg.

Bob and Sibyl become tense

Bob Brownrigg—what would he be writing to me for? He's coming with us, isn't he?
Braun Major Brownrigg is dead.
Bob Dead! But he was here this morning.
Braun So!
Bob He came to say good-bye to my wife and he brought——
Braun Letters?
Bob He brought his wife.
Sibyl (*to Lanz*) Is she all right?
Lanz No. She is very ill.
Sibyl Ill? How can she be ill?
Lanz She has been taken to the hospital on Guernsey.
Braun (*to Bob*) Take off your coat.
Bob Oh now, look here—even if there were some letters, what would I be taking them to Germany for?
Braun Take off your coat.
Bob (*wearily doing so*) O.K., but you won't find anything.

Braun goes through the pockets, finds nothing and throws the coat on the back of the chair

Braun Turn out your pockets.
Bob (*going through them*) Pipe—dried roseleaf tobacco. Nothing. One shirt-tail hankie. Nothing. One spare shirt-tail hankie.
Braun Now, the inside pockets.
Bob Well, there's only one. (*He takes a wallet from his inside pocket*) In here is a photograph of my wife, some money and a letter from my step-son dated March sixth, nineteen forty-one.

Braun puts out his hand for the wallet and Bob angrily slaps it in

Braun (*holding something out*) What's this?
Bob My English driving licence—and it won't be much use to you in the invasion as it's even more out of date.

Braun (*handing back the wallet*) You may go now.
Bob Oh no. I'm not leaving my wife here with you.
Braun (*to Muller*) Nehmen Sie das.

Muller picks up the hold-all and goes to the door

Go. The boat is waiting.
Bob Not until I know what's going on.
Braun Take him away.
Bob Lanz, I'm not leaving my wife here with him.
Sibyl I'll be all right, Bob.
Lanz You must go now, Mr Hathaway. The boat is waiting.
Bob O.K. (*To Braun*) But, before I go, I'll tell you one thing, fella. Harm
    her and I'll track you down when this war's over, and strangle you with
    my bare hands.
Braun The boat is waiting, Mr Hathaway.

Bob turns towards Sibyl

Sibyl No, Bob. We've said good-bye.
Bob Right. (*He turns in the doorway*) Be seeing you.

Bob exits, followed by Muller

(*off*) Keep smiling, Cecile.
Cecile (*off, sobbing*) Yes, Sir.
Bob (*off*) Don't worry. I'll be back.

Sibyl moves to the window

Braun (*to Lanz*) Vernehmen Sie das Dienstmadchen.

Lanz exits

Sibyl turns back from the window

Sibyl Where's Major Lanz gone?
Braun To question your maid.
Sibyl About your fictitious letters?
Braun They are not fictitious, Mrs Hathaway. I find this letter to you in
    the house of Major Brownrigg. (*He takes out a letter*)
Sibyl It's a forgery.
Braun Why do you say that? Why do you assume it is incriminating?
Sibyl I don't.
Braun Then why say that? It might just say "Good-bye", Mrs Hathaway,
    might it not—nothing more?
Sibyl Yes, I suppose it might.
Braun Then why do you suggest it is a forgery?
Sibyl Because you're so worked up about it, it obviously doesn't say just
    that.
Braun You are right. It says—"You have our last messages". In Major
    Brownrigg's handwriting. Would you agree? (*He hands her the letter*)

Sibyl It's forged. (*She sits in the armchair*)

Braun No, Mrs Hathaway. It is not forged as you know very well. It is in Major Brownrigg's writing. Where, then, are these letters?

Sibyl I haven't got any.

Braun What is the meaning of that sentence, then?

Sibyl You know perfectly well that "messages" in English means words spoken and not written. And the messages that Major Brownrigg's talking about in that letter were about the jewellery his wife left here when she came to say good-bye this morning. And she left us an address in England to send them to, if they did not return after the war.

Braun So, where is this jewellery?

Sibyl In my desk.

Braun Let me see it.

Sibyl Certainly.

There is a pause. Braun waits for her to move

It's in the pigeon-hole.

Braun (*going to the desk and finding the jewel-case*) You have no documents or letters?

Sibyl No.

Braun (*taking out an envelope from the case*) This it?

Sibyl Yes. That is the address in England that she wants them sent to if she does not come back.

Braun (*having read it*) This is all you have?

Sibyl Yes.

Braun (*ransacking the desk*) There is nothing more in these drawers?

Sibyl No. You may look if you like.

He finds a locked drawer

Braun You have the key?

Sibyl It's on the ink-tray.

Braun unlocks the drawer and continues to search

That's where I keep the money for the wages.

Braun Nothing else?

Sibyl Nothing but the wages.

Braun finishes searching the desk and returns to the middle of the room

Braun It is not wise to lie to me, Mrs Hathaway. If I should find these letters you will be in trouble.

Von Schmettau enters. He wears a black arm-band

Braun Herr Oberst, I am looking for some letters Major Brownrigg left with Mrs Hathaway.

Von Schmettau So. When?

Braun When he and Mrs Brownrigg came to say good-bye this morning.

Von Schmettau You must let him have these letters, Mrs Hathaway.

Sibyl I haven't any letters. It's all nonsense. Major Brownrigg left no letters. Mrs Brownrigg left her jewellery. I've just shown it to him. But they left no letters. I keep telling him this, but he won't believe me.

Von Schmettau Why is it that you will not believe her, Doctor?

Braun Because of this letter. (*He hands the letter to Von Schmettau*)

Von Schmettau (*reading it*) Mrs Hathaway, in spite of this, you still say that you have no letters?

Sibyl Yes.

Von Schmettau You understand how serious it will be for you if it shall be proved that you are not telling the truth?

Sibyl Yes.

Von Schmettau Have you any letters, Mrs Hathaway?

Sibyl No.

Von Schmettau Any documents of any kind?

Sibyl No. Nothing but the jewellery.

Von Schmettau Are you ready to accept what Mrs Hathaway says, Doctor?

Braun No, Herr Oberst.

Von Schmettau Then you must prove her wrong.

Braun I am about to search this room, Herr Oberst. Then the house then the environments.

Von Schmettau May I suggest you start with the environments? In my experience, people know a house will be the first place to be searched. Look in the stables, Doctor, in the garden sheds, the dog kennels, the rabbit hutches—everywhere in fact. And Major Lanz will no doubt help you. Then, if you find nothing, start again in the house.

Braun Yes, Herr Oberst.

Braun exits

Von Schmettau I am sorry that I could not save your husband from the deportation. I had hoped to. But he too is an enemy now.

Sibyl I know. But thank you for trying.

Von Schmettau I regret it was to no avail. And I am deeply sorry about Major Brownrigg and his wife.

Sibyl What happened? Did he have a heart attack?

Von Schmettau He killed himself.

Sibyl Killed himself—why?

Von Schmettau And Mrs Brownrigg tried to kill herself, too.

Sibyl Oh no.

Von Schmettau She had stabbed herself——

Sibyl Oh!

Von Schmettau —sixteen times.

Sibyl Oh . . .

Von Schmettau But the doctor says she may survive.

Sibyl But why?

Von Schmettau They did not wish to be deported.

Sibyl Well, neither did Bob, but he accepted it.

Von Schmettau He is a younger man. Were they disturbed this morning when they came to see you?

Sibyl No, not outwardly, not that I noticed. But I wasn't all that calm myself, with Bob going. I can't believe it. They were here in this room. They must have been so frightened they didn't know what they were doing.

Von Schmettau Frightened? Of what?

Sibyl Germany. Of going there.

Von Schmettau There is no reason for this.

Sibyl Isn't there?

Von Schmettau No, no, no.

Sibyl That's not what I've heard. What about the concentration camps?

Von Schmettau Fom whom have you heard this?

Sibyl From no-one. I just heard it.

Von Schmettau From whom?

Sibyl Nobody, I tell you.

Von Schmettau You are lucky that you say these things to me, and not to Dr Braun. Be more careful in the future, Mrs Hathaway, if not for your own sake, then for your husband's.

Lanz, Braun and a soldier walk past the windows outside

I think we should change the subject.

Sibyl Yes. By all means. Anyway, I'd like to ask you something.

Von Schmettau Certainly.

Sibyl Is Hitler dead, by any lucky chance?

Von Schmettau No.

Sibyl Then why are you wearing that arm-band?

Von Schmettau My son died on the Russian front last week.

Sibyl Oh, I'm sorry.

Von Schmettau Thank you.

Sibyl Please forgive me.

Von Schmettau Of course.

Sibyl How old was he?

Von Schmettau He was twenty-one. (*He sits*) He was the youngest of my children, and the one I knew best. My wife will be very sad. Still, I go on leave next week, and I will try to comfort her.

Sibyl Was he a soldier too?

Lanz, Braun and soldier are seen briefly again outside

Von Schmettau No, he was not a professional. He was an ornithologist.

Sibyl Oh, how nice.

Von Schmettau The last time that I saw him was on my leave last year. It was his leave too, thank God. And he has photographed this bird— what do you call it—the great-crested—greber . . . ?

Sibyl Grebe.

Von Schmettau Yes, that is right. A grebe's nest. And he has put this hide of camouflage, you understand, beside the water. And, one morning, he say to me, "Father, come down to the water after breakfast and talk to me all the way. And then I enter the hide, and you walk back to the house, alone, still talking. And this grebe will think that I am still with you, because birds cannot count." And it was so. And he has taken the photographs, and they were good. I have one back at my headquarters. How I wish I had it with me. I will bring it the next time I come.

Sibyl Please do.

Lanz and Braun pass the window on their way back

Von Schmettau (*rising*) I have much admired your rabbits, Mrs Hathaway. I paid them a visit on my way from the harbour.

Sibyl (*rising*) But how did you know about—the rabbits?

Von Schmettau Your husband told me. We met on the road. With so many troops about he seemed concerned for their safety, and I promised him that I would see that they were well cared for. (*He takes some letters from his pocket*) I have read these letters, Mrs Hathaway, and they are harmless. None the less, I keep them for you till the search is over.

There is a knock on the door

Herein.

Lanz and Braun enter

Ja?

Braun We find nothing outside, Herr Oberst. Now we search the house with your permission.

Von Schmettau You will carry on, and make sure that you find these letters if you do not wish to find yourself in trouble.

Von Schmettau exits

Sibyl sits and the search begins, as—

the CURTAIN *falls*

PRELUDE TO SCENE 5

"D" Day has come.

Early this morning the Allies began the assault on the north-western face of Hitler's European Fortress.

The Allied Commander-in-Chief, General Eisenhower, has issued an Order of the Day, addressed to each individual of the Allied Expeditionary Force. In it he said:

"Your task will not be an easy one. Your enemy is well trained, well equipped and battle hardened. He will fight savagely. But this is the year 1944. The tide has turned. The free men of the world are marching together to victory.

"I have full confidence in your courage, devotion to duty and skill in battle. We will accept nothing less than full victory. Good luck; and let us all beseech the Blessing of Almighty God upon this great and noble undertaking."

This Order was distributed to assault-elements after . . .

SCENE 5

The same. Summer 1944—a fine day

Sibyl is sitting at breakfast. Cecile enters

Cecile That young soldier's at the door, Madam, with a message for you.
Sibyl By himself—with no officer?
Cecile No, Madam.
Sibyl What is the message?
Cecile He won't tell me, Madam. He wants to see you.
Sibyl Oh well, show him in.
Cecile You haven't finished up your breakfast, Madam.
Sibyl The bread tastes so fishy . . .
Cecile Well, I had to use that salt from the boiled seawater to make it, Madam. That's what it is.
Sibyl Never mind. Our week's ration of proper bread arrives tomorrow.
Cecile Yes, thank goodness, Madam.
Sibyl Show him in, Cecile.
Cecile Yes, Madam. (*She calls through the door*) Come in, please.

Muller enters, Cecile exits

Sibyl Well, what is it?
Muller Major Lanz has sent me, Madam.
Sibyl Why didn't he come himself?
Muller He busy. We stand to this morning, very early.
Sibyl Oh, why?
Muller There is the alarm.
Sibyl A raid, you mean?
Muller I do not know.
Sibyl You do, but you won't tell me. Well, what is the message?
Muller That Herr Oberst von Schmettau come to see you very soon this morning.
Sibyl Then there must have been a raid. He wouldn't come as early as this otherwise.
Muller I do not know.
Sibyl Well, thank you.

Muller moves to the door

Where have you been? I've not seen you for nearly a year.
Muller I go to Germany for a course.
Sibyl Oh. What sort of course?

Muller It was an engineering course.
Sibyl Did you find it interesting?
Muller Ja.
Sibyl Wilhelm Muller—that is your name, isn't it?
Muller So, you remember?
Sibyl I remember everything. There's not much else to do these days. How is Ilse?
Muller She is well.
Sibyl Still faithful to you?
Muller I hope. On my last leave we are married.
Sibyl Oh, how lovely!
Muller And she write last week to say that she begin to have the baby.
Sibyl Oh, how wonderful!
Muller Dankeschön.
Sibyl You'll get some more leave now when the baby's born?
Muller I hope.
Sibyl Of course you will.
Muller I do not know. I hear the rumour that there may be no more leave.
Sibyl Oh, why?
Muller I do not know.
Sibyl Well, let's hope that the rumour's wrong, for your sake.
Muller And your husband—he is well?
Sibyl Yes, thank you, Wilhelm. I had a letter from him last week.
Muller I am glad. I like your husband.
Sibyl Thank you, Wilhelm.
Muller Because he is not afraid. And that is why I like you too. (*He moves over to the table*) Madam, I tell you something that you must not tell to any other person, because if it should be known that I have told you, I am shot.
Sibyl For heaven's sake, don't tell me, then!
Muller I tell you, Madam, because I am trusting you. There is a raid last night. But it is not on Sark. It is on the French coast between Le Havre and Cherbourg. It is the invasion by the British and Americans. Now, I have told you.
Sibyl Thank you, Wilhelm. But you shouldn't have. Never trust a woman with a secret.
Muller I trust you, Madam.
Sibyl Well, I hope you're justified.
Muller I, too, because if not, I am shot.
Sibyl Then, why take the risk?
Muller Because you ask me about Ilse. And I think, if you remember her, then you remember Mr Hathaway much more. And so, I think I give you hope that the war end soon, and he come home.
Sibyl You're a silly sentimental little German boy. But none the worse for that.

He moves back to the door

Muller I go now.

Sibyl Good luck with the baby.
Muller Thank you, Madam.
Sibyl Perhaps you'll get home now before it's born.
Muller That is what I hope.

Muller exits

Sibyl sits at the table, smiling. Then gets up and collects some knitting she is unravelling and goes to the armchair

Cecile hurries in

Cecile What was the message, Madam?
Sibyl The message? Oh, Colonel von Schmettau's coming to see me very soon, that's all.
Cecile That's all, Madam! I was just going to take the floor boards up in the hall to hide the potatoes.
Sibyl Well, you mustn't, now.
Cecile But it's this morning the baker delivers them on his round, Madam.
Sibyl Tell him to postpone it till this afternoon.
Cecile Yes, Madam. Oh, and I'd better tell the cowman not to grind the extra corn this morning, had I?
Sibyl You had, Cecile. Otherwise the Colonel's going to smell a rat. (*She gives an uncharacteristic giggle*) Oh dear, I'm sorry, Cecile—I didn't mean that as a joke.
Cecile What's come over you, Madam?
Sibyl Nothing. Why?
Cecile Your voice sounds happy.
Sibyl Well, it's a beautiful day.
Cecile I've got a headache.
Sibyl Oh, poor Cecile.
Cecile Well, did you hear all those planes going over last night, Madam? They kept me awake.
Sibyl Yes, I did.
Cecile The Second Front's begun, I shouldn't wonder.
Sibyl Do you really think so, Cecile?
Cecile I do, I feel it in my bones.
Sibyl Perhaps that's why you've got a headache.
Cecile And the troops are on alert, they tell me, Madam.
Sibyl Who did?
Cecile The cowman. Oughtn't we to listen to the wireless?
Sibyl Not now. With the Colonel coming.
Cecile Is that all he told you, Madam?
Sibyl Oh, he told me he got married on his last leave . . .
Cecile No!
Sibyl And his wife's expecting a baby.
Cecile Did you ever! Well, life goes on, I must say. Still, he's young enough.

Sibyl Well, he must be twenty. He was seventeen when he first came. Oh . . . (*She laughs*) I was going to say "how time flies". But that's the one thing it doesn't do.

There is the sound of a car approaching. Cecile goes to the window

Cecile Here's the Colonel now, Madam.
Sibyl Show him in, please, Cecile.
Cecile The war won't last much longer, not with all those bombers going over. It can't. We'll have it on the wireless tonight, I'll bet you anything you like, Madam.
Sibyl I won't take you, Cecile. You're too confident.

There is a knock on the front door

Show him in.

Cecile exits

Cecile (*off*) Good morning, Colonel.
Von Schmettau (*off*) Good morning.

Von Schmettau enters

Sibyl Good morning, Colonel. Isn't it a lovely day?
Von Schmettau Good morning, Mrs Hathaway. You have received my message?
Sibyl Yes. You're very early. What's the trouble?
Von Schmettau Trouble?
Sibyl Cecile tells me that there's an alert on.
Von Schmettau How does she know this?
Sibyl From the cowman.
Von Schmettau It is just routine—to keep the troops on their toes.
Sibyl Yes, yes, of course.
Von Schmettau But I have disturbed your breakfast—please forgive me.
Sibyl Dry bread and toasted barley coffee, if you call that breakfast.
Von Schmettau Not luxurious, but adequate.
Sibyl Adequate? Two pounds of bread a week, even for hard-working men —you call that adequate—and only two ounces of meat a fortnight—and all we get is the tails and offal. And no potatoes at all. We're almost starving.
Von Schmettau Almost, but not quite. My directive from the Supreme Command is to cut down your rations to the barest survival level.
Sibyl Well, you've certainly done that.
Von Schmettau No—I allow you more than that by cutting down the rations of the occupation forces.
Sibyl And what good does that do? They just steal our chickens and our calves and pigs—our dogs and cats! You haven't got an army, Colonel— all you've got's a pack of thieves and beggars!

Von Schmettau Men of any nationality are prone to steal when they are hungry. And my men are disciplined when they are caught.

Sibyl With their stomachs full. There are women on the island, who can't feed their babies, they're so undernourished.

Von Schmettau I am aware of that, Mrs Hathaway. And I am sorry for it. But your navy will not allow supplies through.

Sibyl And why should they? To feed you?

Von Schmettau And you. And as for what you say about the bread and the potatoes—this is not true and you know it very well.

Sibyl (*disconcerted, but trying for injured innocence*) I don't know what you're talking about.

Von Schmettau (*firmly*) Then I explain. It has been clear to me for a long time that the corn and the potato crop we commandeer on Sark, falls short of the amount you harvest by a long way. But I overlook your hoarding. There is too the question of more deportations. I have fought against this. My overlords in Berlin insist there be more deportations in order to conserve what food remains here for the occupation forces. I have said it is not necessary. They have said "All right then, if you will have no more deportations then you must cut down the food supplies again." I fight against this too, and so it goes on. Now I fight no more. Instead I come to say good-bye.

Sibyl Good-bye?

Von Schmettau Yes. I have been recalled to Germany.

Sibyl Oh, I'm sorry. I'll miss you. Isn't life extraordinary? Fancy me, an Englishwoman, saying that to you, a German Colonel, in the middle of a war. But it's the truth.

Von Schmettau I say it too.

Sibyl So—you've retired?

Von Schmettau No. I have been dismissed.

Sibyl Dismissed? Why?

Von Schmettau I have not satisfied my masters in Berlin.

Sibyl In what way?

Von Schmettau Why should I bore you with my affairs?

Sibyl No, no. I'm interested. Do sit down, Colonel. You look very tired.

Von Schmettau Thank you. (*He sits, and there is a pause*) Mrs Hathaway, in this war, for a German officer, things have not been so easy.

Sibyl I can understand that.

Von Schmettau Especially for a soldier like myself. I am of the old school, brought up in the military traditions of my country. And that I cannot change. But it makes things very difficult. I wish to do my duty, but, at the same time, I cannot bring myself to do all the things that are expected of me. That is why I am dismissed.

Sibyl What will you do when you get home?

Von Schmettau Hope to survive.

Sibyl Survive? Oh, you mean the bombing?

Von Schmettau No, I do not mean the bombing, Mrs Hathaway.

Sibyl What then.

Von Schmettau Strange things are happening in Germany at this time.

Fellow officers that I have known all my life, disappear—not from the
battlefield—but from their homes, and are not seen again.

Sibyl You mean they're murdered?

Von Schmettau I do not know.

Sibyl Or put in concentration camps.

Von Schmettau Of this I am ashamed. The entire German army is ashamed.

Sibyl That's no good. You must do something.

Von Schmettau What can we do?

Sibyl Throw Hitler out.

Von Schmettau And what would that achieve?

Sibyl A lot. If you did that the Allies would negotiate.

Von Schmettau They have not said so.

Sibyl But, of course they would.

Von Schmettau Then why do they not say so? All that they have said is
that we should surrender unconditionally. And that we cannot do.

Sibyl You'll have to in the end.

Von Schmettau What would your Mr Churchill say if someone should
demand that he surrender unconditionally?

Sibyl I shouldn't like to guess.

Von Schmettau And the German army say the same. The Navy and the
Air Force too. That is why we go on fighting—whether it is Hitler or the
Kaiser or Field Marshal Rommel. It is necessary for our honour that
we go on fighting.

Sibyl But you cannot win. With the Americans against you, you can't win.
You must lose.

Von Schmettau I do not agree.

Sibyl Any day now they'll land in Europe, with the British and the Poles
and the Free-French . . .

Von Schmettau If they do, then we will drive them back into the sea.

Sibyl I doubt it. I've got used to German boasts.

Von Schmettau (*making as if to leave*) I can see no purpose in continuing
with this discussion.

Sibyl (*relenting slightly*) Do you know who your successor will be?

Von Schmettau He is not yet appointed.

Sibyl Oh. You're not going at once?

Von Schmettau Who knows? It depends on the war situation. I came today
because I am on Sark in any case, to see how Major Lanz conducts
himself in the alert. But it is possible I may not come back here before
I am replaced.

Sibyl I see.

Von Schmettau Mrs Hathaway, you must not think that I have said the
things that I have said this morning in the hope that, if your theory is
proved correct and Germany is beaten, you will intercede on my behalf
and say I am not quite so bad a Hun as Attila?

Sibyl (*smiling*) Of course not.

Von Schmettau I say these things because I feel them—passionately.

Sibyl I accept that.

Von Schmettau German soldiers do not like war any more than any other soldiers do. I know it is the fashion to say otherwise—but it is not true. They fight because it is their duty to fight for their country. They cannot do otherwise. You understand that?

Sibyl Yes. Yes.

Von Schmettau, obviously under stress, sits down. Sibyl watches him for a moment

Sibyl I think I'd like a glass of brandy. Would you? (*She gets up and moves towards the study*)

Von Schmettau No—no.

Sibyl (*firmly*) We'll drink your health and Bob's.

Von Schmettau If you insist.

Sibyl I do.

Sibyl exits to the study

Von Schmettau slumps in the chair for a moment, then pulls himself together and straightens his back

Von Schmettau You have heard from your husband?

Sibyl (*off*) Yes, I had a letter from him last week.

Von Schmettau And how is he?

Sibyl (*off*) Not too bad, considering.

Von Schmettau In what part is he?

Sibyl (*off*) Somewhere in Silesia.

Sibyl enters, carrying the brandy and glasses, and goes to the table

Von Schmettau Oh yes, I know it well. (*He moves over to the table*) My wife comes from there.

Sibyl You'll be seeing her soon, won't you?

Von Schmettau I hope.

Sibyl You don't really think you'll be in danger, do you?

Von Schmettau I am much afraid.

Sibyl But can't your uncle help you?

Von Schmettau How is it you know about my uncle?

Sibyl Bob looked you up in the *Almanac de Gotha* when you first came.

Von Schmettau I see. You were impressed, I hope.

Sibyl Tremendously. Surely he can save you?

Von Schmettau It is possible that he may be hard put to save himself. I will tell you something in confidence.

Sibyl Of course.

Von Schmettau My uncle has been worried in his mind throughout the war. He is of the old school too. He say this to my wife: "If Hitler goes to war, I go with him. If Hitler win the war, I win it also. If Hitler lose the war, I lose it too. That is the duty of a soldier. Field Marshals do not overthrow their leaders, Anna Maria. If they do, then they are traitors."

Sibyl But does he still say this?

Von Schmettau He say it to her again on my last leave. And when she say: "Uncle Gerdt, I understand all that, but Hitler's mad", he answer: "I am a field marshal, not a doctor, Anna Maria. It is not for me to diagnose the Fuhrer's mental state, nor to prescribe a cure. My job is to fight off my country's enemies." I wish that you could meet him. He is a great man. And he is much concerned that this dilemma is not understood in England or America. (*He raises his glass*) Your husband's health.

Sibyl And yours.

Von Schmettau And may you soon be reunited.

Sibyl Thank you. And I wish the same for you and your wife.

Von Schmettau Thank you. (*He puts down his glass and turns to her*) I have something that I wish to give you. (*He takes a photograph from his pocket*)

Sibyl What's that?

Von Schmettau It is of the great crested grebe.

Sibyl The great crested . . .?

Von Schmettau The photograph my son has taken.

Sibyl Oh yes, of course. Isn't it good?

Von Schmettau You would like it?

Sibyl No, of course not. It's yours.

Von Schmettau No, no, I have more copies at home.

Sibyl Thank you, that's very kind of you. (*She puts it up on the mantelpiece*)

Von Schmettau I charge you five hundred marks for it.

Sibyl Five hundred marks?

Von Schmettau That is what you owe me for the bombing of Berlin.

Sibyl Oh, yes, of course. I had forgotten. (*She goes over to her handbag on the desk*)

Von Schmettau Oh, then—you knew about the bombings?

Sibyl I mean—I'll have to take your word for it, naturally.

Von Schmettau Naturally.

Sibyl More than London?

Von Schmettau More. Much more.

She gives him the money

Thank you. I shall keep this as a souvenir. And now I say good-bye.

Sibyl I haven't really thanked you for the things you've done to help me—specially since Bob went.

Von Schmettau You are speaking of the little matter of the rabbit hutches?

Sibyl That—and other things. I'm grateful, very grateful, and I shall not forget . . . What did you do to Dr Braun when he couldn't find the letters?

Von Schmettau Nothing.

Sibyl Nothing? But you said he'd be in trouble.

Von Schmettau And now it is I who am in trouble. It is not wise to say anything to such a man as Dr Braun.

Sibyl You mean to say that he reported you?

Von Schmettau One does not know. One knows so little these days. (*He* *moves towards her*) Good-bye, Mrs Hathaway. It has been pleasant knowing you (*He kisses her hand*)

Sibyl Good-bye—and good luck, Count von Schmettau.

Von Schmettau Thank you. I shall need it. (*He salutes, English-fashion and moves to the door*) Did you hear the aeroplanes last night?

Sibyl Yes, they woke me up.

Von Schmettau There were very many of them.

Sibyl So Cecile said.

Von Schmettau British and American.

Sibyl Oh, really?

Von Schmettau What a pity it is that you have not got a wireless set.

Von Schmettau smiles and turns to go, as—

the CURTAIN *falls*

SCENE 6

The same. Summer, 1945

Cecile is alone in the room, dusting. There is a wireless on the table, and strains of "The Water Music" are heard. The music fades. Cecile runs towards the study

Cecile Madam, Madam. (*She runs back to the wireless*)

Sibyl enters and stands by the armchair in the middle of the room

Alvar Liddell (*on the wireless*) This is London. We are interrupting programmes with the great news that Berlin has fallen ...

Lanz comes in from hall and stands listening also

... and that the German armed forces in Italy have surrendered unconditionally to Field Marshal Alexander. The Berlin garrison were forced into surrender after a siege in which more than seventy thousand prisoners have been counted. So ends the battle on which Hitler staked his life and a large part of the German army. It started little more than a fortnight ago with the launching of the Red Army's offensive across the Oder. This produced the Hitler Order of the Day proclaiming that everything had been done to build up the Berlin defences with a mighty array of artillery and countless new formations of reserves. In the last few years the Germans have heard of the capture by their armies of many capital cities—Vienna in nineteen thirty-eight, Prague and Warsaw in nineteen thirty-nine, Copenhagen, Oslo, the Hague, Brussels and Paris in nineteen forty, followed by Belgrade and Athens in nineteen-forty-one. Now, in nineteen forty-five, it's Berlin which has been captured. The Prime Minister will broadcast to the nation at eleven-fifteen.

Strains of "The Trumpet Voluntary". Sibyl turns to Lanz who removes his gun belt and places it on the chair. Sibyl turns quickly back to Cecile

Sibyl We mustn't waste the batteries. (*She switches off the radio*) I'll switch it on again in ten minutes. (*She picks up the telephone which is on the desk*) Hullo—hullo ... (*She jiggles it*) Hullo ... (*She slams it down*) Why is the telephone not connected, Major Lanz?
Lanz I have had no orders that it should be reconnected, Madam.
Sibyl That's not surprising, is it? All your troops in Guernsey must be prisoners by now. For you the war is over, Major Lanz. Kindly see that it is reconnected at once.

Lanz Yes, Madam.
Sibyl Oh, and Cecile, go and get the flags out of the cupboard.
Cecile Yes, Madam.

Cecile exits

Sibyl Major Lanz, see that all your troops are disarmed, before the British troops arrive here.
Lanz Yes, Madam.
Sibyl And the mines round the harbour must all be dismantled.
Lanz That should be done by the engineers, Madam. I have no experts on the island.
Sibyl Too bad. You must make do with what you've got, then. You put them up, so it's up to you to take them down again.
Lanz But the work is dangerous except for experts.
Sibyl I can't help that. British soldiers will be coming over. And I'm not risking an accident.
Lanz No, Madam.

Cecile returns with a folded Union Jack and a Stars and Stripes

Sibyl And get one of your men to run up these flags.
Lanz Yes, Madam. (*He takes the flags from Cecile*)
Sibyl And report to me, by telephone, the minute that the mines are cleared.
Lanz Yes, Madam.

Lanz exits

Cecile Yes, Madam! No, Madam! Hark at him! He doesn't know what's hit him!
Sibyl Neither do I, Cecile—neither do I. What shall we do to celebrate? I know. Let's finish off the last few drops of brandy, shall we? Go and get it, Cecile.
Cecile (*going to the study*) Good idea, Madam.

Cecile exits to the study

Sibyl picks up the phone again

Sibyl Hullo—hullo—operator—hullo—operator . . .

Cecile returns with the brandy

Cecile He won't have had the time yet, surely?
Sibyl (*putting down the phone*) No, I suppose not.
Cecile Just be patient, Madam.
Sibyl Oh, I'm trying to, but it isn't easy. After five years.
Cecile That's true, but it's been worth waiting for.

Sibyl Is there enough?

Cecile Yes, Madam, and a bit more. (*She hands Sibyl a glass*)

Sibyl Thank you, Cecile.

Cecile picks up her glass

To the end of the war, Cecile!

Cecile The end of the war, Madam.

Muller bursts in

Muller They are flying, Mrs Hathaway.

Sibyl What are?

Muller The flags.

Sibyl Oh, thank you.

Muller turns to go

Would you like a drop of this?

Muller Well, just a mouthful. I'm due at the harbour at the double. Major's orders.

Cecile Not the Major's—Mrs Hathaway's. Madam's Commander-in-Chief on Sark now until the soldiers get here. So you'd better put *your* gun on that chair too.

Muller (*doing so*) Yes, Sir!

Sibyl How's the baby, Wilhelm?

Muller Oh, is good—in the last letter. Looks like me, my wife says.

Sibyl Poor child!

Muller (*drinking*) Good health, Major! (*He puts the glass down and runs to the door*)

Cecile Cheeky boy!

Muller Auf Wiedersehn!

Muller exits

Sibyl Well, Ilse will be glad they've surrendered at any rate.

Cecile He didn't look too sad himself.

Sibyl He's young. He's got his whole life before him, Cecile. (*She goes to the telephone again*) Hullo—hullo—hullo . . . This is still not connected.

Cecile And who is it you wish to telephone, Madam?

Sibyl London.

Cecile You're an optimist, Madam.

Sibyl I want to ring the War Office to ask them if they've any news of Mr Hathaway.

Cecile I'd let them ring you, Madam. They'll be busy today. Why not finish off the brandy?

Sibyl No, I mustn't. I'm Commander-in-Chief of all the German forces on Sark.

Cecile So you are, Madam. I was forgetting. Well then, I'd better put the cork in.

Sibyl You have some more if you want to, Cecile.
Cecile No, I shouldn't either—seeing that I'm Second-in-Command.

Sibyl bursts out laughing

Well, aren't I?
Sibyl You are, Cecile. I hereby appoint you Herr Oberst von Cecile!
Cecile Oh, Madam!

There is a knock on the front door

Sibyl See who it is, Cecile.
Cecile Yes, Madam.

Cecile exits

A British Corporal (Robinson) walks past the window. Sibyl suddenly notices him and goes over to the window

Sibyl Hullo . . .
Robinson Blimey, who're you?
Sibyl I'm the Dame of Sark. What's your name?
Robinson (*standing inside the window*) Robinson. Jim Robinson.
Sibyl It's very nice to see you.

Cecile enters with an English Colonel

Cecile Colonel Graham, Madam.
Sibyl (*not hearing and holding out her hand to the Corporal*) How do you do?
Robinson I'm fine thanks. Well, how's the weather been?
Sibyl It's varied.
Cecile Madam.
Robinson (*seeing Colonel Graham and standing to attention*) Sorry, Sir.
Sibyl (*turning*) Oh . . .
Graham Mrs Hathaway?
Sibyl Yes.
Graham Colonel Graham, Ma'am. John Graham.
Sibyl (*coming forward*) I'm so sorry. Please forgive my rudeness.

Graham salutes and shakes hands

How do you do. And this is Cecile.
Graham Hullo, Cecile.

Graham shakes hands with Cecile

I've a telegram here for you, Mrs Hathaway. (*He gives it to her*) It says your husband's fit and well, I'm glad to say.
Sibyl (*opening it*) How wonderful!
Cecile Does it say when he'll be home, Madam?
Sibyl No, Cecile. I expect he's still in Germany. But he's well—and that's all that matters. (*To Graham*) And the others who were deported?

Graham I expect there'll be some news in a day or two. I can't tell you how relieved I am to find you all right, Mrs Hathaway.

Sibyl Why shouldn't I be all right?

Graham We thought there might have been trouble, as we couldn't get through to you on the telephone.

Sibyl We've had no trouble, have we, Cecile?

Cecile No, Madam. None at all.

Sibyl I took command, you see, immediately after the surrender.

Graham So the German major told me.

Sibyl You've met Major Lanz?

Graham Yes, on his way down to the harbour. He asked me to tell you that the telephone is working now.

Sibyl Good.

Graham And that the mines will be cleared soon.

Sibyl Better still.

Graham notices the gun and rifle on the chair, and smiles

Graham I can see that you've already held a partial surrender ceremony!

Sibyl Yes. And I told Major Lanz to see that everybody else's arms were handed in.

Graham They were stacked on the quay when I arrived. (*He laughs*) I'm beginning to wonder, 'Was my journey really necessary?'

Sibyl Well, of course it was, if only to bring me this.

Graham Oh yes. But otherwise you haven't left me much to do.

Sibyl Except to have a glass of brandy?

Graham Thank you.

Sibyl Cecile, get two more glasses, will you?

Cecile goes to the study

Can your soldier have some?

Graham Why not? If there's enough to spare.

Robinson Thank you, Sir.

Sibyl There's not much, but I think it'll just about do.

A distant explosion is heard. Robinson goes outside the window

Sibyl (*pouring brandy*) Cecile, Colonel Graham says his soldier can have one too. Call him, would you please? His name's Robinson. (*She gives Graham a glass*)

Cecile Yes, Madam. (*She goes to the window with two glasses*) Robinson— we've got a glass of brandy for you.

Robinson Jolly good. Thanks, love.

Robinson takes the brandy and stands in the window

Sibyl (*to Graham*) What's the time? Oh, we're forgetting Mr Churchill. (*She runs to the wireless*) You don't mind, do you? (*She switches the wireless on*)

Graham No, I'd like to hear it. (*To Robinson*) Robinson, come in, you should hear this. (*To Sibyl*) May he?

Sibyl Of course.

Churchill (*on the wireless*) . . . the cease-fire began yesterday to be sounded all along the fronts, and our dear Channel Islands are also to be freed today. The German war is therefore at an end. Advance Britannia— Long Live the Cause of Freedom—God Save The King.

Sibyl turns off the wireless

Sibyl The King. (*She looks at Cecile*) "Our dear Channel Islands" . . .

The telephone suddenly rings

Oh! (*She jumps, then laughs*) I'm so sorry. I haven't heard a telephone for years. (*She picks up the receiver*) Hullo . . . Oh yes, Major Lanz? . . . A soldier? What . . .? . . . One of ours? . . . But he's only just left here. What happened? Was there a fight? . . . A mine . . . The English Colonel's here. I'll ask him. (*She turns to Graham, obviously deeply upset*) A young German soldier's been killed by a mine down at the harbour. Major Lanz wants to know if he can fire a volley over his grave.

Graham It sounds most irregular. May I speak to him?

Sibyl hands the receiver to Graham and moves to the centre of the room

(*on the phone*) Major Lanz? . . . It's Colonel Graham speaking. Get Sub-Lieutenant Richards to speak to me, will you? He's the naval officer in charge of my boat.

Sibyl (*half to herself*) I gave the order. I'm responsible.

Graham Someone would have given it, sooner or later.

Sibyl Major Lanz said it was dangerous. I insisted, though.

Graham And quite right, too. If it hadn't been a German, it could very well have been one of ours.

Sibyl He was my friend . . .

Graham (*into the phone*) Richards? . . . Colonel Graham here. What's all the hurry about burying this fellow? . . . Oh, the transport's waiting to leave, is it? . . . Well, you can let Lanz fire off his volley over the boy's grave, so long as you keep a close eye on the whole operation. Right? (*He hangs up*)

Sibyl It goes on, Colonel Graham. It goes on. When will it ever stop?

the CURTAIN *falls*

FURNITURE AND PROPERTY LIST

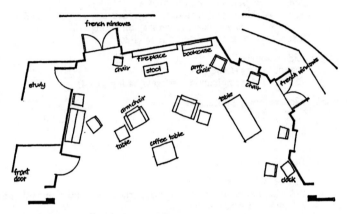

SCENE 1

On stage: 2 armchairs
2 high-backed chairs
Desk chair
2 occasional tables. *On them:* ashtrays
Firestool
Coffee table. *On it:* game of patience set out
Dining table
Desk. *On it:* writing materials, ink-tray with key to locked drawer in it, telephone. *In drawers:* blank cards, dressing, jewel-case with envelope (in locked drawer). *Below it:* wastepaper-basket
Bookshelves. *In them:* books, including *Almanac de Gotha*, tobacco tin
Bell by fireplace
Carpet
Window curtains

Off stage: 2 books (Bob)
Briefcase containing poster (Braun)

Personal: Bob: pipe, matches

SCENE 2

Strike: Books

Set: Chairs to original positions
Forms and writing materials on table
Patience cards for fresh game
Tobacco pouch in bookcase

Off stage: Tray with brandy and 2 glasses (Bob)

SCENE 3

Strike: Brandy, glasses, tray
            Patience cards
            Sibyl's papers

Set: Tobacco pouch back in bookcase
            Almanac de Gotha back in bookcase
            Breakfast things for 2, including 2 cups, saucers, teaspoons, coffee-pot,
                milk jug, small plates, all on tray on dining table
            2 small chairs in position at dining table

Off stage: Rifle (Muller)
            List of houses (Lanz)
            Basket of chrysanthemums, scissors, string (Sibyl)

Personal: Muller: family photo

SCENE 4

Strike: Basket, scissors, string

Set: Pair of Bob's gloves by fire
            Bob's hold-all on floor. *In it:* various articles of clothing and toiletries,
                packet of razor-blades
            Jewel-case and letter in desk pigeon-hole
            Key in desk ink-tray

Off stage: Packet of letters (Schmettau)

Personal: Bob: tobacco pouch, pipe, 2 shirt-tail handkerchiefs, wallet with
                money, letter, photograph, driving licence
            Braun: letter
            Schmettau: black arm-band

SCENE 5

Set: Desk tidy
            Breakfast tray for one on dining table
            Knitting and needles on desk
            Sibyl's handbag on desk, containing money—500 marks

Off stage: Tray with brandy and 2 glasses (Sibyl)

Personal: Schmettau: photograph of great crested grebe

SCENE 6

Strike: Breakfast tray
            Knitting
            Brandy and glasses

Off stage: Union Jack and Stars and Stripes flags (Cecile)
            Tray with brandy and 3 glasses (Cecile)
            Telegram (Graham)
            2 brandy glasses (Cecile)

LIGHTING PLOT

Property fittings required: brackets, lamps (dressing only), fire effect
Interior. A drawing-room. The same scene throughout

SCENE 1   Day
To open: General effect of warm summer daylight. Fire out
No cues

SCENE 2   Day
To open: General effect of spring daylight. Fire out
No cues

SCENE 3   Day
To open: General effect of autumn morning light. Fire out
No cues

SCENE 4   Day
To open: General effect of cold winter light. Fire lit
No cues

SCENE 5   Day
To open: As Scene 1. Fire out
No cues

SCENE 6   Day
To open: As Scene 1. Fire out
No cues

EFFECTS PLOT

SCENE 1

No cues

SCENE 2

Cue 1 **Bob:** ". . . but you mustn't."   (Page 15)
Sound of car approaching and stopping

Cue 2 **Bob** takes out tobacco pouch   (Page 17)
Sound of car leaving

SCENE 3

No cues

SCENE 4

No cues

SCENE 5

Cue 3 **Sibyl:** ". . . the one thing it doesn't do."   (Page 47)
Sound of car approaching and stopping

SCENE 6

Cue 4 As CURTAIN rises   (Page 53)
*Handel's "Water Music" on radio, followed by: Alvar
    Liddell announcement, followed by: the "Trumpet
    Voluntary"*

Cue 5 **Sibyl** switches off radio   (Page 53)
Music off

Cue 6 **Sibyl:** ". . . it'll just about do."   (Page 57)
Distant explosion

Cue 7 **Sibyl:** "Of course."   (Page 58)
Churchill announcement on radio

Cue 8 **Sibyl** switches off radio   (Page 58)
Voice off

Cue 9 **Sibyl:** ". . . 'Our dear Channel Islands' "   (Page 58)
Telephone rings

Lightning Source UK Ltd.
Milton Keynes UK
UKOW01f0611310715

256123UK00001B/13/P